English Touring Theatre and
Liverpool Everyman & Playhouse
present the world première of

THE ODYSSEY:
MISSING PRESUMED DEAD

by Simon Armitage

First performed on 25 September 2015
at the Everyman theatre, Liverpool

LIVERPOOL EVERYMAN & PLAYHOUSE

Two Great Theatres
One Creative Heart

We are two distinct theatres, almost a mile apart, which together make up a single artistic force.

For over 10 years we have been driven by our passion for our art form, our love of our city and our unswerving belief that theatre at its best can enhance lives. While our two performance bases could hardly be more different, they are united by our commitment to brilliant, humane, forward-thinking theatre that responds to its time and place.

At the beating heart of the theatres is our work with writers; since it is our passionate belief that an investment in new writing is an investment in our theatrical future. Our mission is to nurture and develop the playwrights who will represent the city's talent, its voice and its unique energy, while at the same time showcasing new work by established local, national and international playwrights. In the last 10 years we have produced 38 world premières across the two theatres, 35 of them were by Liverpool writers. Of these, 10 were debut plays and 15 of the productions toured or transferred.

It's an exciting time for new writing at the Everyman & Playhouse. Our wide-ranging support for writers includes an annual Young Writers' Programme; a Writers on Attachment scheme; Our Playwrights Programme; and our festival of new work and ideas, *Everyword*. And most wonderfully, the new Everyman has a Writers' Room where writers can work, research and meet to ferment ideas.

For more information about the Everyman & Playhouse, including the full programme and activities such as playwright support visit **everymanplayhouse.com** or call **0151 709 4776**

  @LivEveryPlay   EverymanPlayhouse

Liverpool Everyman & Playhouse are a registered charity (1081229) and gratefully acknowledge the support of our funders, donors and audiences.

 ARTS COUNCIL ENGLAND   Liverpool City Council

**ETT
ENGLISH
TOURING
THEATRE**

English Touring Theatre is one of the UK's most successful and exciting production companies. At the heart of everything the company does is the passionately held belief that people throughout the country expect and deserve theatre of the very highest quality imagination and ambition.

**A MAD WORLD
MY MASTERS**
Spring 2015

ARCADIA
Spring 2015

TWELFTH NIGHT
Autumn 2014

ETT IN NUMBERS

22 Years
1.6 Million Audience Members
727,650 Minutes of Theatre
1.3 Million Touring Miles
1,600 Creatives, Designers and Performers

"English Touring Theatre is surely the national theatre of touring."

Sir Ian McKellen, patron

ABOUT US

Supported using public funding by
**ARTS COUNCIL
ENGLAND**
LOTTERY FUNDED

ett.org.uk

Cast (in alphabetical order)

Lee Armstrong	Magnus / Ensemble
Simon Dutton	Prime Minister / Tiresias / Cyclops / Ensemble
Roger Evans	McGill / Eurylochus
Polly Frame	Anthea / Athena
David Hartley	Kite / Ensemble
Ranjit Krishnamma	Reynolds / Ensemble
Chris Reilly	Fenton / Perimedes / Ensemble
Sule Rimi	Soli / Polites / Ensemble
Danusia Samal	Leader of the Opposition / Circe / Anticlea / Briseis / Ensemble
Colin Tierney	Smith / Odysseus
Susie Trayling	Penelope

Company

Writer	**Simon Armitage**
Director	**Nick Bagnall**
Designer	**Signe Beckmann**
Lighting Designer	**Mike Robertson**
Composer	**James Fortune**
Sound Designer	**Jennifer Tallon-Cahill**
Movement & Fight Director	**Kev McCurdy**
Casting Directors	**Jerry Knight-Smith CDG** and **Anne McNulty CDG**
RTYDS Assistant Director*	**Sarah Van Parys**
Costume Supervisor	**Jacquie Davies**
Dialect Coach	**Hugh O'Shea**
Production Manager	**Felix Davis**
Company Manager	**Sarah Lewis**
Company Stage Manager (Tour)	**Bo Barton**
Stage Manager (Liverpool)	**Gemma Dunne**
Deputy Stage Manager (Liverpool & Tour)	**Roxanne Vella**
Asst Stage Manager (Liverpool)	**Gemma Gale**
Asst Stage Manager (Tour)	**Daniel Hampton**
Dresser (Liverpool)	**Laura Hollowell**
Wardrobe Supervisor (Tour)	**Daphne Bates**
Lighting Programmer (Liverpool)	**Andy Webster**
Stage Technician (Liverpool)	**Mike Cantley**
Relighter (Tour)	**Adam Mottley**
Touring Fit-up Electrician (Tour)	**David Moorcroft**
Set Construction	**Harrogate Theatre Scenic Services**
Stage Engineering	**The Scenery Shop**

For this production, the company would like to thank
Tash Holdaway, Kevin Reynolds and Damien Parkinson

*Three-Month Placement at Liverpool Everyman & Playhouse through
the Regional Theatre Young Director Scheme

Cast

LEE ARMSTRONG
Magnus / Ensemble

Theatre credits include: *War Horse* (National Theatre/tour); *Talk Show* (Royal Court); *Brilliant Adventures* (Royal Exchange, Manchester) and *Events While Guarding The Bofors Gun* (Finborough Theatre).

Television credits include: *Midsomer Murders*, *Inspector George Gently* and *Doctors*.

SIMON DUTTON
Prime Minister / Tiresias / Cyclops / Ensemble

Theatre credits include: *A Marvellous Year for Plums* and *The Rehearsal* (Chichester Festival Theatre); *Woyzeck* (Edinburgh Festival); *The Merchant of Venice* (Royal Shakespeare Company); *Not About Heroes* (National Theatre); *Present Laughter* (Birmingham Rep); *Endgame*, *Pygmalion* and *Nothing* (Citizens Theatre, Glasgow); *Nothing* (Theatre Brits off Broadway/New York); *Journey's End* (national tour); *Private Lives*, *An Ideal Husband*, *Gaslight*, *A Doll's House*, *Ghosts*, *Boeing Boeing*, *The Winslow Boy* and *Hamlet* (Clwyd Theatr Cymru).

West End credits include: *Lady Windermere's Fan* (Albery Theatre); *Plague Over England* (Duchess Theatre) and *Another Country* (Queen's Theatre).

Television credits include: *The Saint*, *Doctor Who*, *Not Going Out* and *Dracula*.

Film credits include: *Memed My Hawk*, *King David*, *Dangerous Beauty*, *Walking with the Enemy*, *1911* and *A Royal Christmas*.

ROGER EVANS
McGill / Eurylochus

Theatre credits include: *Britannia Waves the Rules* (Royal Exchange, Manchester); *Henry VI* (Shakespeare's Globe); *Salt Root and Roe* (Donmar Warehouse/Trafalgar Studios); *Cloak Room* (Sherman Cymru); *The Fixer* (High Tide Theatre); *Fast Labour* (Hampstead Theatre/West Yorkshire Playhouse); *Box* (Live Theatre, Newcastle); *Woyzeck* (St Anne's NY/Gate Theatre); *Professor Bernhardi, Rose*

Bernd (Oxford Stage Co/Arcola); *How Love Is Spelt* (Bush Theatre); *Art and Guff* (Soho Theatre/Sgript Cymru); *Everything Must Go* (Sherman Theatre); *Gas Station Angel* (Royal Court, international tour); *Scum and Civility* and *The Man Who Never Yet Saw Woman's Nakedness* (Royal Court, international festival).

Film credits include: *Black Mountain Poets*, *Tarzan*, *Svengali*, *Kubricks*, *Hunky Dory*, *Ghosted*, *Abroad*, *Cow*, *A Bit of Tom Jones*, *Daddy's Girl*, *Atonement*, *All or Nothing*, *Human Traffic*, *Suckerfish* and *Bourne Identity*.

Television credits include: *Da Vinci's Demons*, *Gittins*, *New Tricks*, *The Warm-Up Guy*, *Fallout*, *Venezuela Blues*, *Midsomer Murders*, *Goldplated*, *Ghostboat*, *Aberfan*, *Sea of Souls*, *Casualty*, *Doctors*, *Murphy's Law*, *Absolute Power*, *Nuts and Bolts*, *The Bench*, *Bradford in My Dreams*, *Sleeping with the TV On*, *A Mind to Kill*, *Rhinoceros*, *Syth*, *Crime Traveller*, *The Bill* and *Wonderful You*.

Radio credits include: *One More Question*, *Foursome*, *Station Road* and *The Member of Penbanog*.

POLLY FRAME
Anthea / Athena

Polly trained at Bristol University.

Theatre credits include: *Mermaid* (Shared Experience); *Arcadia* (Tobacco Factory); *Pastoral* (Soho Theatre); *After Miss Julie* (Young Vic); *The Crossing 66 Books* (Bush Theatre); *The Comedy of Errors* (Stafford Shakespeare Festival); *Earthquakes in London* (National Theatre); *The Count of Monte Cristo* (West Yorkshire Playhouse); *Macbeth* (Chichester Festival Theatre, West End and Broadway); *Home-Work* (Bodies in Flight for Singapore Esplanade); *Twelfth Night* (Filter); *The Prime of Miss Jean Brodie* and *Poor Mrs Pepys* (New Vic); *AC/DC* (Royal Court); *Cleansed* (Arcola); *Who by Fire* and *Skinworks* (Bodies in Flight) and *Seven and a Half Minutes of Happiness*, *Di-sect* and *Eve* (Bristol Old Vic).

Television credits include: *Man Down*, *The Tunnel*, *Coronation Street*, *Holby City*, *Doctors*, *The Curse of the Hope Diamond*, *Silent Witness*, *EastEnders*, *Bunny Town*, *Sea of Souls*, *Accused*, *Life Begins*, *New Tricks*, *Meet the Magoons*, *The Giblets* and *Servants*.

Film credits include: *Macbeth*, *Half Light* and *Duplicity*.

DAVID HARTLEY
Kite / Ensemble

David trained at the Central School of Speech and Drama

Theatre credits include: *Henry VI, Parts 1, 2 and 3* (Shakespeare's Globe); *As You Like It* and *Merlin* (Grosvenor Park); *Billy Liar* (West Yorkshire Playhouse); *Cling to Me Like Ivy* (Birmingham Rep); *The Tempest* (York Theatre Royal/Sprite Productions); *I Caught Crabs in Walberswick* (High Tide Festival); *Lovely and Misfit* (Trafalgar Studios); *If I Were You* (Stephen Joseph Theatre, Scarborough); *Holes* (Nuffield Theatre, Southampton); *Measure for Measure* (Shakespeare's Globe/ USA tour) and *Edward II* (Sheffield Theatres).

Television credits include: *Holby City, Doctor Who, Doctors, The Bill, Talk to Me, Kingdom* and *The Amazing Mrs Pritchard.*

Radio credits include: *Noble Cause Corruption* and *Flare Path.*

RANJIT KRISHNAMMA
Reynolds / Ensemble

Theatre credits include: *Behind the Beautiful Forevers, Dara* and *Playing with Fire* (National Theatre); *Boy with a Suitcase* (Arcola Theatre); *Measure for Measure* (Reckless Endeavour); *Mistaken* (Vayu Naidu); *Three Sisters* (Messiaen Productions); *The Daughter* (The Wedding Collective); *Passage to India* (Shared Experience); *Othello* (Nottingham Playhouse); *Midnight's Children* (Royal Shakespeare Company); *A Midsummer Night's Dream* (Attic Theatre Company); *Life of Padmasambhava* (Namsay Dorje, San Francisco); *The Exhibitionist* (Ridiculusmus, European tour); *The Last Yellow* (Chelsea Centre); *A Clockwork Orange* (Northern Stage); *The Castle* (Moving Being); *World Storytime* (Theatre Royal Stratford East) and *Barbarians* (Old Red Lion).

Television credits include: *The Life and Adventures of Nick Nickelby, Casualty, Silent Witness, Law and Order, Doctors, Coming Up: Would Like To Meet, EastEnders, Harley Street, New Street Law, Little Britain, Grease Monkeys, Murphy's Law, Waking the Dead, Into the Void, The Bench, Holby City, The Kidnap, The Bill, The Turnaround, Little Napoleons* and *Tender Loving Care.*

Film credits include: *A Hundred Streets, Blitz, A Good Sharma, The Last Horror Movie, High Heels and Low Lives, New Years Day* and *Shooters.*

CHRIS REILLY
Fenton / Perimedes / Ensemble

Chris graduated from Royal Welsh College in 2009.

Theatre credits include: *Let the Right One In* (National Theatre of Scotland); *Truth and Reconciliation* (Royal Court); *.45* (Hampstead Theatre); *Love Your Soldiers* (Sheffield Theatres) and *In My Mouth* (Theatro di Picollo Milan).

Film credits include: *Everest* and *Allies.*

Television credits include: *Game of Thrones, Call the Midwife, Moving On, Atlantis, Our World War, Suspects, Shetland, Silent Witness, Homefront, EastEnders, Doctors, Crash,* as well as over thirty voice credits in productions such as *Macbeth, Brave* and *The Hobbit.*

SULE RIMI
Soli / Polites / Ensemble

Theatre credits include: *The Rolling Stone* (Royal Exchange, Manchester/ West Yorkshire Playhouse); *Boarder-game* (National Theatre Wales); *Downtown Paradise* (Welsh Fargo Theatre Company); *Othello* (Fluellen Theatre Company); *Muscle* (Shock n Awe); *Serious Money* (Walking Exploits); *New Arrivals* (Sherman Theatre Company); *Do Mice Think Bats are Angels?, Othello* and *Victory* (Ugly) and Rude: *A Ska Musical* (Give It a Name).

Film credits include: *Black or White, The Adventurer: Curse of the Midas Box, Silent Night, Bloody Night: The Homecoming, The Machine, Elfie Hopkins and The Gammons, Night of The Living Dead: Ressurection, Panic Button, Little Munchkin, Robinson Crusoe, Webbed, Going Dutch, Visitors Visa, The Gatekeeper, Colonial Gods, Be Kind Rewound, Rock 'n' Roll Killers, The 'I' Inside, Playhouse, Heart, Out of Nowhere, Starter for Ten, Phalure Inc.* and *Francis.*

Television credits include: *Unforgotten, DNN, Stella, Crash, Caerdydd, Scrum IV: Operation, Bobble, Casualty, Dr Who, Scrum IV, Fondue, Sex and Dinosaurs, The Story of Tracey Beaker, First Degree, Outside the Rules* and *The Black Lion.*

DANUSIA SAMAL
Leader of the Opposition
Circe / Anticlea / Briseis
Ensemble

Theatre credits include: *The Broker* (Young Vic); *How to Hold Your Breath* (Royal Court); *The House that Will Not Stand* (Tricycle Theatre); *Circles* (Birmingham Rep/Tricycle Theatre); *Billy the Girl* (Clean Break/Soho Theatre); *The Birthday Party* (Royal Exchange, Manchester); *1001 Nights* (Unicorn Theatre/Transport); *Liar Liar* (Unicorn Theatre); *The House of Bernarda Alba* (*A Mother's Will*) (StoneCrabs); *After the Rainfall* (Curious Directive); *Street Scene* (The Opera Group, Young Vic) and *The Suit* (Joined Up Thinking @ The Young Vic).

Film credits include: *In Close Quarters* and *Do You Want to Try Again?*

Television credits include: *Tyrant* (Series 2).

Radio credits include: *Doctor Who*, *Acquitane*.

COLIN TIERNEY
Smith / Odysseus

Credits for the Everyman & Playhouse: *The Misanthrope*, *Tartuffe*, *Our Country's Good* and *Lady of Leisure*.

Other theatre credits include: *The Father* (Theatre Royal Bath/Tricycle Theatre); *Britannia Waves the Rules*, *The Seagull* and *Cold Meat Party* and (Royal Exchange, Manchester); *The Last Days of Troy* (Royal Exchange, Manchester/ Shakespeare's Globe Theatre); *Betrayal* and *Hamlet* (Sheffield Crucible); *Hedda Gabler* (Theatre Royal Bath and tour); *One Minute* (Courtyard Theatre); *Paul*, *Guiding Star* and *The Machine Wreckers* (National Theatre); *How Love Is Spelt* (Bush Theatre); *Duchess of Malfi* (Royal Shakespeare Company); *Hamlet* (Bristol Old Vic); *Death of Cool* (Hampstead Theatre); *Othello* (National and world tour); *Ivanov* and *The Life of Galileo* (Almeida); *Henry VI* (Royal Shakespeare Company Tour); *Look Back in Anger* (Plymouth); *No Remission* (Tour) and *Sienna Red* (Peter Hall Company).

Television credits include: *Vera* (Series 4), *Silent Witness*, *Holby City*, *DCI Banks*, *Garrow's Law*, *New Tricks*, *Casualty*, *1909*, *Waterloo Road*, *The Bill*, *Inspector Lynley*, *The Walk*, *Island at War*,

Serious and Organised, Foyle's War, The Vice, Mersey Beat, Tough Love, Midsomer Murders, Casualty, Soldier Soldier, Between the Lines, Mad and Sandy, Cracker, An Unsuitable Job for a Woman and McCallum.

Film credits include: Nowhere Boy, Splintered and Bye Bye Baby.

Radio credits include: Sparkling Cyanide, Antony and Cleopatra, The Last Dare and Macbeth.

SUSIE TRAYLING
Penelope

Credits for the Everyman & Play-house: Arthur Miller's The Hook

Other credits include: The Crucible and Twelfth Night (West Yorkshire Playhouse); Thomas Tallis (Shakespeare's Globe); Idomeneus and Vanya (Gate); The Seagull (Manchester Library Theatre); Sons Without Fathers (Belgrade Theatre/ Arcola Theatre); King John, Richard III and A Soldier in Every Son (Royal Shakespeare Company); The Constant Wife, Private Lives and The Waters of the Moon (Salisbury Playhouse); Antony and Cleopatra (Nuffield Theatre); Mary Goes First and The Mob (Orange Tree); Love's Labour's Lost (Rose Theatre); A Doll's House, The Portrait of a Lady, Habeas Corpus and Measure for Measure (Peter Hall Company);

Women of Troy, Dream Play, Iphigenia at Aulis and The Forest (National Theatre); Don't Look Now (Sheffield Lyceum/Lyric Hammersmith); Skylight (Stephen Joseph Theatre); The Importance of Being Earnest and Closer (Royal & Derngate, Northampton); Camera Obscura (Almeida); Hamlet (Northcott Theatre); Edward II (Sheffield Crucible) and Anna Karenina (Bolton Octagon, nominated for Best Actress, Manchester Evening News Awards).

Television credits include: Midsomer Murders, Vera, The Bill, Holby City, We'll Take Manhattan, Doctors, Emma, Heartbeat, Casualty and The Inspector Lynley Mysteries.

Film credits include: Fragile, Fog Bound and All The Queen's Men.

Company

SIMON ARMITAGE
Writer

Simon Armitage is a poet, playwright, novelist and broadcaster. He was born in 1963 in the village of Marsden and lives in West Yorkshire. He has recently been appointed Professor of Poetry at Oxford University.

His poetry collections include Book of Matches (1993), The Dead Sea Poems (1995), Tyrannosaurus Rex Versus the Corduroy Kid (2006) and Paper Aeroplane (2015). He has written two novels, Little Green Man (2001) and The White Stuff (2004), as well as a bestselling memoir All Points North (1998). In

2012, he published *Walking Home*, a *Sunday Times* bestseller which chronicled his 264-mile walk along the Pennine Way. His latest work is *Walking Away* (2015), where he swaps the moorland uplands of the north for the coastal fringes of Britain's south-west.

Simon also writes for radio, television, film and stage. He is the author of four stage plays, including *Mister Heracles*, a version of Euripides' *The Madness of Heracles*. He has presented films for BBC4 on *Sir Gawain and the Green Knight*, Arthurian literature and on the *Odyssey*, sailing from Troy in Turkey to the Greek island of Ithaca.

He has received numerous awards for his poetry, including the Sunday Times Author of the Year, a Forward Prize, a Lannan Award, and an Ivor Novello Award.

NICK BAGNALL
Director

Nick is the Associate Director of the Liverpool Everyman & Playhouse.

Credits for the Everyman & Playhouse: *A Midsummer Night's Dream* and *The Electric Hills*.

Other theatre credits include: *I Am Not Myself These Days* (Pleasance); *The Last Days of Troy* and *Britannia Waves the Rules* (Royal Exchange, Manchester); *The Death of King Arthur* and *Sir Gawain and the Green Knight* (Shakespeare's Globe); *Henry VI Parts 1, 2 and 3* (Shakespeare's Globe/UK tour); *A Christmas Fair* and *A Midsummer Night's Dream* (Milton Rooms, Malton); *Fragile* (Belgrade Theatre); *Betrayal* (Crucible Theatre); *A Separate Reality* (Royal Court); *By Jeeves* (Landor); *Billy Liar* (West Yorkshire Playhouse); *Guys and Dolls* (Arts Theatre, Cambridge); *Entertaining Mr Sloane* (Trafalgar Studios); *Burning Cars* (Hampstead Theatre); *Mongoose* (Assembly Rooms, Edinburgh); *Promises and Lies* (Birmingham Rep); *Bolthole*, *'Low Dat* (The Door, Birmingham Rep) and *The Ruffian on The Stair* (Old Red Lion).

SIGNE BECKMANN
Designer

Signe trained at the Motley Theatre Design Course.

Theatre credits include: *Sunspots* and *The Glass Supper* (Hampstead Theatre Downstairs); *Crave* and *4.48 Psychosis* (Crucible Studio, Sheffield); *Ghosts* (New Vic); *The Distance* (Orange Tree); *Debris* (Southwark Playhouse); *A Handful of Stars* (Trafalgar Studios); *Molly Sweeney* (Lyric Belfast/The Print Room); *Land of Our Fathers* (503/ Trafalgar Studios); *There Has Possibly Been An Incident* (Royal Exchange, Manchester); *Larisa and the Merchant* (Arcola); *The Thing About Psychopaths* (Red Ladder); *Comedy of Errors* (Cambridge Arts Theatre); *American Justice* (Arts Theatre, West End); *The Serpent's Tooth* (Almeida/Shoreditch Town Hall); *Insufficiency* (Riverside Studios); *Peep* (Pleasance, Edinburgh); *Benefactors* (Sheffield Theatres); *The Glee Club* (Hull Truck); *The Knowledge* and *Little Platoons* (Bush Theatre); *Crawling in the Dark* (Almeida Projects); *Ghosts* (Young Vic); *King Ubu* (Corona La Balance, Denmark) and *Dancing at Lughnasa* (Aubade Hall, Japan).

Opera credits include: *Don Giovanni* (Royal Danish Opera, costume design); *The Turn of the Screw* (Opera Up Close); *La Serva Padrona* (Sa de Miranda, Portugal); *Volume* (ENO Opera Works, Sadlers Wells) and *Eugene Onegin* and *Giasone* (Iford Arts).

Dance credits include: *Gameshow* (Company Chameleon, The Lowry); *Quiproquo* (Rapid Eye, Denmark) and *Meridan* and *Phantasy* (Rambert Company, Queen Elizabeth Hall).

Screen credits include: *The Club*, *Plan B – Killa Kela*, *Centrepoint* and the Headlong Theatre 2013 Season Trailer.

MIKE ROBERTSON
Lighting Designer

An Olivier Award Winner for *Sunday in the Park with George* (Menier Chocolate Factory/ Wyndhams Theatre) and a What's On Stage Design award nominee for his design for *On the Waterfront* (Theatre Royal Haymarket).

Recent credits include: *Great Expectations* and *James and the Giant Peach* (Dundee Rep); *Jacques Brel Is Alive and Well*, *Dear World*, *Keeler*, *Six Actors in Search of a Director* and *The Billie Holiday Story* (Charing Cross Theatre); *Go See* (Kings Head); *Propaganda Swing* (Nottingham/Coventry); *Toast* and *The Dead Wait* (Park Theatre); *Joe Stilgoe, Songs on Film* (Edinburgh); *Songs for a New World* (Guildford); *Cirque Berserk* (Tour); *1001 Nights* (Saudi Arabia); *Piano Piano* (Cottiers); *Hairspray* (Kuala Lumpur/Singapore); *Volcano* (Vaudeville Theatre and UK tour);

Funny Peculiar (UK tour); *Dry Rot* (UK tour); *Parade* (Old Vic Tunnels); *Gibraltar* (Arcola Theatre); *Fragile* and *The Father* (Belgrade Theatre, Coventry), *Murder on the Nile* (UK tour); *Verdict* (UK tour); *Larkrise to Candleford* (UK tour); *Riccardo Primo* (Royal College of Music); *The Producers* and *Seesaw* (Arts Ed); *Death and Gardening* (UK tour, Edinburgh Festival); *Oedipus* (Nottingham Playhouse/Edinburgh Festival); *Third Floor* (Trafalgar Studios); *Company* (Southwark Playhouse); *Billy Liar* (West Yorkshire Playhouse); *Cabaret* (Wilton's Music Hall); *Guys and Dolls*, *My Fair Lady* and *Anything Goes* (Cambridge Arts Theatre); *Educating Rita* (Watermill Theatre, Newbury); *Wolfboy* (George Square Theatre, Edinburgh); *New Boy* (Trafalgar Studios); *Hair* (English Theatre, Frankfurt); *Too Close to the Sun* (Comedy Theatre); *Five Guys Named Moe* (English Theatre, Frankfurt); *Othello* (Birmingham Stage Company); *Sit and Shiver* (Hackney Empire); *Deathtrap* (English Theatre, Frankfurt); *The Spring Proms* (Royal Albert Hall); *Fascinating Aida* (UK tour); *The Glee Club* (Bolton Octagon/ Cochrane Theatre) and *The Wood Demon* (Playhouse Theatre).

JAMES FORTUNE
Composer

Credits for the Everyman & Playhouse: *A Midsummer Night's Dream*.

Other theatre credits include: *The Rolling Stone* (Royal Exchange, Manchester); *Teh Internet Is Serious Business* and *A Short History of the Royal Court* (Royal

Court); *Posh* (Royal Court/West End); *The Beautiful Cosmos of Ivor Cutler* (Vanishing Point/National Theatre of Scotland); *Dick Whittington and His Cat*, *Jack and the Beanstalk* and *Secret Theatre Show 1* (Lyric Hammersmith); *Our Big Land* (Romany Theatre Company) and *Coffee* (Pleasance, Edinburgh).

James is currently working on the boxing musical *Journeyman* and developing *Lord of the Darts*, the second piece in his sporting musical trilogy.

Awards: Best Music and Sound Critics Award for Theatre in Scotland (CATS) for *The Beautiful Cosmos of Ivor Cutler* (Royal Court).

Television credits include: *Objects of Desire* (Sky Arts).

Radio credits include: *Carmen* by Dan Allum (Radio 4).

As a singer and flautist he has worked with, among others, Tom Jones, Barry Adamson, Kate Nash and Blondie.

James is a founder member of, and arranger for, award-winning vocal harmony band The Magnets. They have appeared on *The Review Show*, *Comic Relief*, *Parkinson*, GMTV, BBC *Proms in the Park* and *Blue Peter* as well as sessions for Radio 1 and 2.

JENNIFER TALLON-CAHILL
Sound Designer

Jennifer has worked for the Liverpool Everyman & Playhouse for 21 years and is Head of Audio-Visual.

Sound designs for the Everyman & Playhouse include: *Educating Rita* (Associate), *Held*, *Proper Clever*, *The Price*, *Tartuffe* (tour re-sound only), *Much Ado About Nothing*, *Billy Liar*, *Season's Greetings*, *The Tempest*, *By the Rivers*, *Homeland*, *Write Now '9*, *Here I Come*, *The Rise and Fall of Little Voice*, *Caravan*, *Twelfth Night*, *Elsie and Norm's Macbeth*, *Shirley Valentine*, *Bouncers and Shakers*, *Rebecca*, *Dead Heavy Fantastic* and *Kissing Rough*.

KEV MCCURDY
Fight Director

Theatre credits include: *'13'*, *The Beaux' Stratagem* and *The Motherf***er with the Hat* (National Theatre); *Marat Sade*, *Julius Caesar*, *Much Ado About Nothing*, *The Jew of Malta*, *Love's Labour's Lost*, *Love's Labour's Won* and *Othello* (Royal Shakespeare Company); *The Heart of Robin Hood* (Royal Shakespeare Company world premiere/Norway/Sweden); *To Kill a Mockingbird* (Royal Exchange, Manchester); *The Last Days of Troy* (Royal Exchange Manchester/Shakespeare's Globe); *Mogadishu* (Royal Exchange, Manchester/Lyric Hammersmith/UK tour); *A View from the Bridge* (UK tour); *Batman Live* world arena tour (world premiere, UK and USA tour); *Troillus and Cressida* and *Romeo and Juliet* (UK, Europe, USA tour); *Hamlet* (world tour); *King Lear* (UK/Middle East tour); *The Taming of the Shrew* (UK/Europe tour); *The Lightning Child* (world premiere); *Julius Caesar*, *The Changeling* and *The Frontline* (world premiere); *The Duchess of Malfi*, *Bedlam*, *The Malcontent*, *The*

Comedy of Errors, *The Knight of the Burning Pestle*, *Measure for Measure* and *The Oresteia* (Shakespeare's Globe); *The House That Will Not Stand* (world premiere); *Broken Glass* and *Multitudes* (Tricycle Theatre); *Miss Saigon* (West End world premiere) and *Sweeney Todd* (West End UK premiere).

Film credits include: *John Carter of Mars*, *Season of the Witch*, *Hunky Dory*, *Set Fire to the Stars*, *Canaries* and *Just Jim*.

Television credits include: *Stella*, *Hinterland*, *Doctor Who Christmas Special*, *Torchwood*, *Becoming Human*, *Belonging*, *Being Human*, *High Hopes*, *The Story of Tracy Beaker*, *Hearts of Gold*, *Carrie's War*, *Pobol Y Cwm*, *Y Pris*, *Caerdydd*, *Pen Taler*, *Gwaith Cartref*, *Alys*, *CCTV*, *Camelot*, *Baker Boys*, *Switch*, *Hollyoaks*, *Hollyoaks after Dark*, *Textual @ttraction*, *Ellen*, *Bitch*, *Arthur's Dyke*, *A Way of Life*, *Arwyr* and *Colonial Gods*.

Opera credits include: *Woyzeck*, *Die Fledermaus*, *Rigoletto*, *Don Giovanni*, *Lulu*, *Tristan und Isolde*, *Carmen* and *Sweeney Todd* (Welsh National Opera); *Tristan und Isolde* (Longborough Opera Festival) and *The Cunning Little Vixen* (Glyndeborne Opera House).

Video games include: *Alien Isolation* and *Everybody's Gone to Rapture* (Sega).

Music videos include: *The Lover of the Light* (Mumford & Sons), *War with Heaven* (Louis Mattrs), *Circles* (I See Monstas), *They Don't Know* (Disciples) and *Mojito* (Kayla).

JERRY KNIGHT-SMITH CDG
Casting Director

Jerry has worked in theatre casting for the past eighteen years. He is Casting Director and an Associate Director at Manchester's Royal Exchange Theatre, where he also cast Simon Armitage's *The Last Days of Troy* with Nick Bagnall. He is a Creative Associate for English Touring Theatre and has also cast freelance for theatre companies across the UK and abroad.

ANNE MCNULTY CDG
Casting Director

Anne was Casting Director at the Donmar Warehouse for twenty years, where she cast more than 100 productions.

Theatre credits include: *Carmen Disruption* (Almeida Theatre); *Outside Mullingar* (Ustinov Studio, Bath); *The Cripple of Inishmaan* (also Cort Theatre, NY); *A Midsummer Night's Dream* and *Henry V* (Michael Grandage Company); *Betrayal* (UK casting, Ethel Barrymore Theatre, NY); *Macbeth* (Manchester International Festival/New York Armory); *Tartuffe* and *Of Mice and Men* (Birmingham Repertory Theatre); *Venice Preserved* (Spectator's Guild); *Good People* (Hampstead Theatre/Noël Coward Theatre) and *Afterplay*, *Translations* and *Wonderful Tennessee* (Crucible Theatre, Sheffield).

As casting consultant: *El Train: Three Plays by Eugene O'Neill* (Hoxton Hall).

SARAH VAN PARYS
RTYDS Assistant Director

Sarah has recently completed the Everyman & Playhouse Young Directors Scheme and is currently on a Three-Month Placement at Liverpool Everyman & Playhouse through the Regional Theatre Young Director Scheme

Credits for the Everyman & Playhouse: *Chair* and *Forever and Anon.*

Other credits include: *New Dawn Fades* (All Roads Meet, UK tour); *Committed* (Liverpool Irish Festival, Lantern Theatre); *The Road to Skibbereen* (Write Now Festival, Unity Theatre/Edinburgh Fringe Festival, with Bee Loud and Straylight Australia); *Inference* (Organised Chaos, King's Arms); *Trolley Shaped Bruise* (Makin Arts, Unity Theatre); *The Morning After* (The Annexe Writers, The Lantern Theatre); *Liverpool and the Titanic* (Theatre in the Rough) and *Pipedreams* (Falling Doors Theatre, Lantern Theatre).

Sarah has also recently set up her own theatre company, Falling Doors Theatre.

The Odyssey: Missing Presumed Dead

Simon Armitage was born in West Yorkshire and is Professor of Poetry at the University of Sheffield. A recipient of numerous prizes and awards, he has published eleven collections of poetry, including *Paper Aeroplane: Selected Poems 1989–2014* and his acclaimed translation of *Sir Gawain and the Green Knight* (2007). He also writes extensively for television and radio and is the author of two novels and the non-fiction bestsellers *All Points North* (1998), *Walking Home* (2012), and *Walking Away* (2015). His theatre works include *The Last Days of Troy*, performed at Shakespeare's Globe in 2014. In 2010 he received the CBE for services to poetry and in 2015 was appointed Professor of Poetry at Oxford University.

SIMON ARMITAGE

The Odyssey
Missing Presumed Dead

FABER & FABER

First published in 2015
by Faber and Faber Limited
74–77 Great Russell Street
London WC1B 3DA

First published in the US in 2016

Typeset by Country Setting, Kingsdown, Kent CT14 8ES
Printed in England by CPI Group (UK) Ltd, Croydon CR0 4YY

A CIP record for this book is available from the British Library

ISBN 978-0-571-32920-5

The Odyssey: Missing Presumed Dead was a co-production by English Touring Theatre and Liverpool Everyman and Playhouse. It was first performed at the Everyman Theatre, Liverpool, on 25 September 2015, prior to a national tour. The cast was as follows:

P.M. / Zeus Simon Dutton
Anthea / Athena Polly Frame
Smith / Odysseus Colin Tierney
Penelope Susie Trayling
Magnus Lee Armstong
Soli / Polites Sule Rimi
McGill / Eurylochus Roger Evans
Fenton / Perimedes Chris Reilly
Kite David Hartley
Reynolds / Barkeeper Ranjit Krishnamma
Circe / Anticleia / Briseis Danusia Samal

Director Nick Bagnall
Designer Signe Beckmann
Lighting Mike Robertson
Composer James Fortune
Sound Jenny Tallon-Cahill
Casting Directors
    Jerry Knight-Smith CDG, Anne McNulty CDG

Characters

P.M. / Zeus
the Prime Minister / the supreme god

Anthea / Athena
the P.M.'s daughter: his senior aide / the goddess Athena

Smith / Odysseus
a cabinet minister / the King of Ithaca

Penelope
his wife

Magnus
their son

Soli / Polites
a government official / Odysseus' first lieutenant

McGill / Eurylochus
Smith's old friend / a crew member

Fenton / Perimedes
England football fan / a crew member

Kite *and* **Reynolds**
journalists

Polyphemus
Cyclops

Circe
a sorceress

Anticleia
Odysseus' mother

Tiresias
a blind ghost and visionary

The Leader of the Opposition

Barkeeper
the owner of a bar in Istanbul

Briseis
his daughter

THE ODYSSEY
MISSING PRESUMED DEAD

Prologue

Athena (*reading from the prologue to* The Odyssey)

Remind us, Muse, of that man of many means,
sent spinning the length and breadth of the map
after bringing the towers of Troy to their knees;

of the lessons he learned in strange cities and towns,
and the heartbreak he suffered, roaming the seas
to land his shipmates and salvage his life.
Of the torture and grief,

of worlds he encountered, battles he fought,
of comrades of his who were sometimes true
and sometimes false, sometimes friends and
sometimes fools . . .

Memory's child, daughter of Zeus,
where to start this story is yours to choose.

*After finishing her recitation, Athena takes off her
classical robes and reveals herself as Anthea, in
modern dress.*

Act One

The Prime Minister's office. The Prime Minister is at his desk. Enter Anthea.

P.M. The numbers, please.

Anthea They're holding up.

P.M. What does 'holding up' mean exactly?

Anthea They're steady. Haven't risen, haven't dipped.

P.M. Flat, then. Flat-lining.

Anthea That's when you're dead. We're two points ahead in a couple of polls, one in another, about level in the rest.

P.M. Level isn't good enough. We need a bit of a heart massage. A bit of fluffing up. Get us over the line.

Anthea It's a month till the election, we just need to hold our nerve. No slip-ups. Leave that to the other lot – they're perfectly capable of self-destruction.

P.M. This football match tonight. Explain.

Anthea Do I look like a sports' fan?

P.M. You're my eyes and ears, my darling. My feet on the ground. So I can keep my mind on higher matters.

Anthea We're playing Turkey.

P.M. We?

Anthea Really? England. In Istanbul. Win and we're through to the World Cup. Lose and we're out.

P.M. And will we? Win?

Anthea In the lap of the gods.

P.M. Hmm.

Anthea We're favourites, apparently, but only just.

P.M. Are we . . . represented?

Anthea Not officially.

P.M. Hmm. I want someone there.

Anthea Bit late, isn't it?

There is a knock at the door.

P.M. No I don't think it is. Come!

Enter Smith.

Here he is. Our man of the people.

Smith Just on my way to the station, sir. So unless it's urgent . . .

P.M. Looking forward to the game tonight?

Smith Certainly am. I've booked the TV room and the beers are in the fridge.

P.M. Ah, you northerners and your beers.

Smith Exactly, and it's five hours on the train, so unless you want to talk about sticking with the false number ten or reverting to a flat back four . . .

P.M. You've got one of those big screens, I suppose?

Smith Big enough. But it runs on paraffin, electricity not having reached our dark corner of the planet. So if you don't mind, sir, I need to get back to start rubbing sticks together so I can light the fire.

P.M. All very well those big screens but better to watch the real thing, wouldn't you say? Better in the flesh?

Smith Everything's better in the flesh.

P.M. Agreed. So it's all there in that envelope: flights, transfers, hotel, some briefing notes on your Turkish equivalent – there's a meet-and-greet at the airport and a little pre-match reception. No beers though, they're a bit funny about all that.

Smith I'm not going to Turkey tonight.

P.M. We need someone there.

Smith I'm Transport and Communication. Send Hennessy. He's Sport and Culture.

P.M. And he's very good on the culture, swanning around the Venice Biennale, mincing through Covent Garden in his purple dinner jacket. But when it comes to sport he doesn't know a football from a whoopee cushion. We need someone a bit more . . . red-blooded.

Smith I'm not going. It's my son's birthday tomorrow.

P.M. He'll have other birthdays.

Smith This is his eighteenth.

P.M. So he's had lots of birthdays already.

Smith I missed them as well.

P.M. In case it had slipped your mind there's a general election coming down the pipe. We need to do a bit of flag-waving. Bask in a bit of national pride and free publicity.

Smith So why don't you go?

P.M. Don't be absurd. Me at a football match – they'd see right through it. Anyway, what if they lose? How would that make me look?

Smith Cheers.

P.M. But you . . . you could deal with it. Take one for the team – isn't that the expression?

Smith I'm not going anywhere.

P.M. That might turn out to be quite a prophetic remark.

Smith What's that supposed to mean?

P.M. You were in the army long enough. You know about duty to the cause.

Smith I was in the Navy.

P.M. Tanks, boats, jets . . . You learnt some discipline and respect is the point I'm making.

Smith They taught me how to bite my tongue till I was sick of the taste of it. Am I being offered the same menu?

Anthea Let's keep this on a professional level, shall we?

P.M. Listen, Smith. You're ambitious. Successful.

Anthea Popular.

P.M. In some quarters. Get your priorities right. Are you really passing up an important career opportunity for a bowl full of custard and a game of pass the parcel?

Smith It's his eighteenth.

P.M. So he'll be grown-up about it. Take it like a man. Well?

Pause.

Smith I haven't got my passport.

P.M. In the envelope. Ink's still a bit wet. And there's a toothbrush.

Smith Money? Translator? Guidebook? Bodyguard?

P.M. Soli will be going with you.

Anthea No, he can't. I mean, he's interpreting for the Egyptian trade delegation this weekend.

P.M. Find a replacement. All set then?

Smith I want the first flight back in the morning.

P.M. Late afternoon I'm afraid. We need you to show your face at a mosque the following day, hands across the water and all that, don't want it to look like you've just been on a free junket. And the connections aren't great, but I expect you're used to that, getting back to those regional airports.

Smith Anything else?

P.M. Smile. We'll be watching.

Exit Smith.

Anthea Will we be watching?

P.M. I've got something on at the club. But send the result.

Anthea You'll be the first to know.

P.M. By the way, how popular?

Anthea People like him.

P.M. Which people? Like him how much?

Anthea I don't know, it's . . . anecdotal. We haven't broken down the data.

P.M. Break it down. Get me some facts. And give your old man a peck on the cheek before you disappear.

She kisses her father on the forehead.

What's the point of nepotism if you can't get a kiss from your favorite daughter?

Anthea I was the best candidate by a mile.

P.M. That you were, my darling, that you were. It's in the blood.

Smith and Soli at the airport.

Soli We need to board, sir.

Smith One more minute.

Soli They'll be closing the doors.

Voice on PA This is a final call for passengers Smith and Soliman flying to Istanbul. Will passengers Smith and Soliman please make their way to the gate immediately.

Soli Sir?

Smith (*on phone*) Penny, it's me again. I'm really sorry. I've phoned Magnus, explained the situation, that it's work and I've got no choice, and that I'll make it up to him. I'm sure he'll understand. (*Whispering.*) Listen, this doesn't change anything. Everything I said, those promises I made about wanting to be at home, with you. Nothing's changed, I swear, you're everything to me. All I ever wanted, all I'll ever want.

Soli Sir –

Smith Let me know you've got this message. Please.

Soli Sir –

Smith (*on phone*) I've got to go – I'll call again later.

Voice on PA Will passengers Smith and Soliman please make their way to the gate immediately, the flight is ready for departure.

Smith dials another number. As the phone rings, we see his elderly mother asleep in a chair. She wakes, makes her way towards the phone, which stops ringing just as she is about to pick it up. She returns to her chair.

Smith Shit bollocks fuck.

Soli After you, sir.

SCENE THREE

P.M. at his club drinking and chatting with old pals. The scene is overlaid with commentary from the football match in the voice of the BBC's senior commentator.

Commentator Only seconds left now, surely. England happy just running the clock down. It hasn't been pretty or particularly convincing but it's been effective. There was a lot of nervousness tonight: supporters, team, management, even up here in the press box – a lot of tension with so much at stake, and a lot of doubt. Any moment now those players out there can start dreaming about taking their place on football's biggest stage. And there is the final whistle. Jubilation from the English fans over to my right. Jeers and whistles from the Turkish crowd. There are some missiles being thrown already and the riot police are making their way on to the pitch to escort the players off and keep the fans in their own sections. A tense atmosphere here, the Turkish manager and coaching staff surrounding the referee and berating the officials, plenty of hand gestures, they'll feel hard done by with some of the decisions tonight, especially the penalty, and also the sending off which turned the whole course of the game. Some ugly scenes here. But it's finished Turkey nil, England one, and England are going to the World Cup. Back to you in the studio.

The sound of the angry crowd carries on in the background, with the strains of 'En-ger-land, En-ger-land, En-ger-land' somewhere within it.

A waiter whispers the result in P.M.'s ear. P.M. nods approvingly.

P.M. Waiter. Champagne all round.

SCENE FOUR

A small side-street bar in Istanbul. Enter Smith, Soli and McGill. An older Turkish man and his daughter, Briseis, are working behind the bar.

Smith In here. This will do.

Soli They're expecting you at the embassy. There are several Turkish diplomats attending and two ministers. It's a good photo opportunity.

Smith Just a quick one.

Soli The ambassador's wife has cooked a whole salmon.

Smith How do you know these things?

McGill That was ace. That was so ace, man. Cheers, man.

Soli Could I have the jacket and tie back now, please?

Smith Well, I couldn't leave you standing outside the ground, could I?

McGill £500 for a ticket? Those touts were having a laugh. Too rich for my blood. How did you recognise me?

Smith You were voted Cumbria's Ugliest Man six years on the trot. No one can forget a face like that.

McGill Salt of the earth this feller. In a box with the VIPs as well – wait till I tell the lads at home. Who did you say I was?

Smith Junior Minister for Fisheries and Agriculture. Paul Halibut. I'm not sure they believed me.

McGill Seriously, man, really appreciate it. And it's great to see you. Surprised you even remember me, now that you've moved up in the world.

Smith You know what they say. All our futures are behind us.

McGill Nah, don't get it.

Smith No, I don't think I do either, just read it on a subway wall.

McGill Oh aye. When was the last time you were in a subway?

Smith Let's have a drink before I get dragged off to this soirée.

McGill The ambassador's drinks reception, eh? Ferrero Rocher on cocktail sticks. How the other half live.

A rowdy group of England supporters enter the bar, including Fenton. They are swathed in flags and Fenton's face is painted with the flag of St George. Singing the theme tune to The Great Escape *they do a conga round the bar, then sit down. One of them drapes a scarf around Smith's neck.*

Fenton (*to Briseis*) One bottle of your strongest poison and five little glasses, sweetheart.

Briseis looks to her father, who nods his permission. Fenton leaves a pile of screwed-up bank notes on the bar.

You do the maths and bring me the change, yeah? Funny fucking money.

Soli (*to Smith*) We should probably go.

McGill My round. It's the least I can do.

Soli Not for me.

Smith How are you getting home?

McGill Kip in the airport then fly back first thing. Don't suppose you've a spare seat on your private jet.

The football fans start singing.

England Fans (*singing, to the tune of 'Go West'*) One nil, to the En-ger-land, one nil, to the En-ger-land, one-nil, to the En-ger-land, one nil, to the En-ger-land.

Soli The car's on its way.

Fenton (*in the direction of the bar*) We'll have another bottle.

Barkeeper We are closed.

Fenton You're what? What are you?

Barkeeper We are closed.

Fenton Well, it don't matter none, cos we're still open over here.

He produces a bottle of vodka from his jacket pocket and pours a round of shots.

Smith I'll just have a quiet word.

Soli I don't think so, sir.

McGill I'm with him. You know what they say round our way.

Smith What do they say?

McGill Never stick your cock in a beehive.

Smith I've never heard anyone say that.

McGill That's because you're out of touch, man. Haven't got your ear to the ground.

The Barkeeper goes over to the group.

Barkeeper Not allowed. We are closed now, you leave.

Fenton Well. that's not very charming is it, not very charming at all. Bad loser I reckon.

Barkeeper Own drink not allowed.

England Fans (*singing*) No surrender, no surrender, no surrender to the Al-Qaeda. No surrender, no surrender, no surrender to the Al-Qaeda.

Barkeeper You go now, please. We are closed.

One of the group takes the Barkeeper's hat and starts throwing it around. The Barkeeper tries to get it back.

England Fans (*singing*)
Oh I'd rather be a Paki than a Turk.
Yes I'd rather be a Paki than a Turk.
Oh I'd rather be a Paki
Or a Nip in Nagasaki
Oh I'd rather be a Paki than a Turk.

Smith Alright, that's enough.

Soli (*holding him back*) Don't even think about it.

Briseis has gone over to the table. When she can't get her father's hat back she takes the bottle of vodka from the table and begins walking away with it. Fenton catches the back of her headscarf and pulls it from her head, at which her father throws a punch at Fenton and a fight breaks out. Smith, McGill and Soli pile in. Sound of breaking glass.

SCENE FIVE

The Prime Minister's bedroom. The small hours. A mobile phone rings at the side of the bed.

P.M. (*anwering phone*) What? What? Wait a minute. (*He turns on a light.*) Tell me again. Where? You have to be joking. Jesus fucking Christ. When? Am I hearing this correctly?

Still on the phone he puts on a dressing gown and walks through to his office, where Anthea is on the other end of the line.

Who's with him?

Anthea Soli, and some old school friend he bumped into at the match, and another guy – we're not sure.

P.M. Why wasn't he at the Embassy?

Anthea Stopped for a drink on the way there.

P.M. Jesus fucking Christ Almighty. I want this sorting out right now before the press get on to it. Who knows?

Anthea We're not sure.

P.M. This is the problem, you see. Leopards and their spots. He might have swapped his donkey jacket for a collar and tie but he's still as vulgar as they come, underneath. Men like him – full of urges, no control.

Anthea He was a Navy commander, he's a self-made millionaire and he's got an IQ of a hundred and thirty-five. He's hardly the village idiot.

P.M. Can't go out of the country without starting a fucking war.

Anthea Well, at least you won't have to worry about his popularity any more, not once this gets out.

P.M. Really? There's probably a sizeable minority out there who quite like the fact that a government minister has been throwing punches in a Turkish bar. Who quite like the idea of an Arab with a bloody nose.

Anthea So what's the worry?

P.M. The worry is that the marginally more enlightened section of the electorate whose pockets we have to piss in aren't going to be rushing to the polling stations to vote for a party with a racist hooligan sitting at the top table. Anyway, this isn't going to get out.

Anthea Too late. It's all over the networks. (*Looking at her phone.*) Oh no. Oh dear God.

P.M. Show me. (*Looking at the phone*). I can't see without my glasses. Get it up on the screen.

Anthea You're not going to like this.

P.M. Put it up there. Let me see.

The still black-and-white photo on the screen shows the girl in the bar with a bleeding wound to her neck, and Smith leaning over her with the broken vodka bottle in his hand and an England scarf around his neck.

Anthea It's from a security camera in the bar.

P.M. He wouldn't have. Would he? Would he?

Anthea No. I mean . . . I don't think so. No.

P.M. Well, he just did, apparently. He's a barbarian. It's in his bones. Is she . . .

Anthea Alive?

P.M. Muslim, I was going to say.

Anthea I'm guessing she is. We don't know anything else.

P.M. Can't we kill it? Delete it? How many what-nots has it had?

Anthea Hits? (*She checks the feed.*) Three.

P.M. Only three – we can squash that, can't we?

Anthea Three million. And counting.

P.M. Perfect. Just perfect. Rabid nationalism, Islam, alcohol, a high-ranking politician, violence against a woman and a forthcoming election. If only he'd had his cock out as well – that would have been a full house, don't you think?

Anthea So what now?

P.M. Get everybody in and tell them to bring their bulletproof vests and shitproof umbrellas. Contact the family up in . . . Northcumberlandshire or whatever. Middle of the night there, I suppose.

Anthea Cumbria. I think you'll find they're in the same time zone as we are.

P.M. I very much doubt it. Still in the fucking stone age if this is anything to go by. And some coffee. Please. And some numbers. Get me some numbers.

SCENE SIX

To a background of sirens and shouting, Smith, Soli, McGill and Fenton are running through the streets of Istanbul. They have been chased towards the docks.

Soli Down here.

Fenton Does he know where he's going?

Smith Where are we, Soli?

Soli No idea.

Fenton It's a fucking dead end, that's what it is.

McGill Is that water down there?

Fenton (*to Soli*) Thanks for nothing, mate. Now look at the shit we're in.

Soli And whose fault is that? You and your little army.

Fenton We were only mucking around. Can't take a joke, can you – had to come steaming in.

McGill Is it the river?

Smith We're on the dockside. It's the sea.

Fenton Should have stayed there with my boys, gone toe to toe. Never one step backwards – that's our motto. Anyway, whose side are you on?

The noise of the chasing mob increases.

Soli Sir?

Smith In we go.

McGill Whooooaa. Hold on a minute. In there? No way.

Smith We've got no choice. It's sink or swim time.

McGill I can't.

Smith Course you can. Don't think about it – just jump.

McGill Can't swim, I mean. I can't swim.

Smith You can't swim?

McGill I'm a farmer. Why would I need to swim?

Smith You live in the *Lake* District.

McGill It doesn't rain that much. Oh, I see what you mean.

Fenton I'm with sheepshagger here. Never one step backwards. (*He walks towards the noise.*) Come on, you fucking scum. I'll take you all on. Every fucking one of ya!

The baying of the following mob rises in response to Fenton's challenge. Fenton turns round and takes a running jump off the end of the pier.

Leg it!

McGill I can't. I'll drown, man. I'll sink like a stone.

Smith Soli?

Soli Hold you breath and close your eyes.

Soli grabs hold of McGill, rushes him to the end of the pier and over the edge, with McGill screaming as they fall. Smith stands alone on the pier. The shouting of the mob and the wailing of the sirens gets louder and louder. For a few seconds he is caught in the glare of a flashlight before walking to the end of the pier, throwing his jacket and tie on the floor, and diving into the darkness.

SCENE SEVEN

The Smith family home in Cumbria. Early morning. Penelope is weeping quietly to herself, looking out of a window.

Magnus Mum? Mum?

Penelope Wait a minute.

Magnus (*entering the room*) You see the photograph?

Penelope I . . . Yes. I did.

Magnus Did he call?

Penelope No.

Magnus Why didn't he call?

Penelope Maybe his phone doesn't work out there.

Magnus Don't shit me. He's got the best phone in the world, even the posh kids at that stupid posh school you send me to haven't got that one. Probably works on Mars – you can probably call God on that phone.

Penelope (*under her breath*) Let's hope so.

Magnus So why hasn't he called?

Penelope He left a message yesterday.

Magnus That was before he bottled a woman in the jugular. Did you call him?

Penelope Only about a thousand times. Did you call him?

Magnus Yes.

Penelope And?

Magnus Just . . . the usual. Leave a message blah blah blah.

The sound of a helicopter landing outside on the lawn. The draught makes the curtains blow in at the window.

Penelope (*looking out*) That didn't take long.

Magnus Who is it?

Penelope The powers that be.

Magnus The Prime Minister.

Penelope As near as dammit.

Magnus Cool flying suit. Shall I show her in?

Penelope If you're happy to land a helicopter on someone's front lawn without permission you're unlikely to ring the doorbell and wait for an answer. See what I mean.

Anthea walks in through the French windows.

Anthea Beautiful place you have here. Very impressive from the air. Thirty acres is it? More?

Penelope This is my son, Magnus.

Anthea He has his father's eyes.

Magnus Hello, I'm in the room, you can address me directly.

Penelope He has his father's mouth, too. Magnus will you make some tea, please?

Magnus Because I'm the butler now?

Anthea Coffee for me. Very kind of you.

Magnus barges out of the room.

Penelope And?

Anthea Has he called? Emailed? Texted? Messaged in any way?

Penelope Nothing.

Anthea So you know as much as we do. Have you talked to the press?

Penelope I only woke up a couple of hours ago, switched the news on and . . . there he was.

Anthea They're going to be all over you. I'll organise security at the gate. Anything you can't handle just ping it on to us.

Penelope Is it real? The photograph?

Anthea You tell me.

Penelope What does that mean?

Anthea We can look into the technology, the authenticity and so on. But when it comes to him . . . is he a violent man?

Penelope No.

Anthea Would he hit a woman?

Penelope No.

Anthea Is he rough in bed?

Penelope Only on request.

Anthea Ten years in the military. He must know how to handle himself.

Penelope He was a high-ranking naval officer.

Anthea I think we both know that spotless white uniform was only for parades and dinner parties. In reality he was a lot darker and dirtier than that. Where did he serve?

Penelope I don't know.

Anthea Yes you do. The Gulf. He'll have enemies.

Penelope He might have friends.

Anthea Very true. Do you recognise the woman in the photograph?

Penelope No. How could I?

Anthea You know what sailors are like. Girl in every port.

Penelope I think you should leave now.

Anthea To be honest we're . . . struggling with this. We need the full picture. Everything. Anything.

Penelope Are you actually trying to help him?

Anthea You're a smart woman, Penelope. He's toxic at the moment, and there are some in the party who think we should just wash our hands of him. Dump him. But I'm not one of them.

Penelope And your father?

Anthea He's a hard-nosed politician. But he's not a tyrant.

Magnus enters with the coffee.

Anthea (*standing to leave, taking a cup of coffee with her*) Do you mind if I have this to go? Oh, and I nearly forgot.

She hands Magnus a wrapped gift.

Happy birthday. Must fly.

Exit Anthea.

Magnus What did she say?

Penelope You heard everything, you were standing behind the door.

Magnus But what did it mean?

Penelope I thought she'd come with answers but it was all questions.

Magnus Do you trust her?

Penelope Against my better judgement . . . I think I might. What's the present?

Magnus (*unwrapping the gift*). Brilliant, because that's exactly what I want right now, some ancient fucking poem.

Penelope Don't use that language in front of me. Your dad wouldn't stand for it.

Magnus Well he isn't here, is he, as per usual.

Penelope This is different.

Magnus Different how? Because this time he might be lying dead in a gutter somewhere – is that what you mean? While we sit here with coffee and poetry.

Penelope Magnus.

Magnus What?

Penelope Happy birthday.

SCENE EIGHT

Smith, now as Odysseus, emerges from the water and climbs into a boat. One at a time, McGill, Soli and Fenton also drag themselves aboard, now transformed into Eurylochus, Polites and Perimedes respectively. They raise the sail of the ancient vessel, extend the oars, and strike out to sea.

SCENE NINE

London. A press conference later in the day.

P.M. As you're all well aware, there was an incident last night in Istanbul involving a member of this government. We're obviously taking it very seriously indeed, but I do have to stress that right now we have no way of verifying any of the details or corroborating those stories and images currently circulating on social media and being reported by the more trigger-happy news-gathering organisations. Certainly Smith attended the international football fixture yesterday evening – many congratulations to our national team by the way, a terrific result and a great boost for the country – er, and appears to have been present when an incident took place in a café in the old part of the city in which a young woman was hurt. It goes without saying that we deplore violence of any kind; our thoughts are with that woman and her family, obviously, and we're working very closely with the Turkish authorities to establish a clearer understanding of events.

Reynolds Was he at the match of his own accord or in an official capacity?

P.M. Oh, I think we all know that Smith is very much his own man, and a very passionate follower of football.

Kite (*interrupting*) Have you seen the photograph?

P.M. (*pressing on*) At this point there is very little substantive information, and please be assured that when anything more does come to light we'll be ready to act upon it and take the necessary steps. Thank you very much.

Reynolds With the election less than a month away, how would you categorise this? A minor embarrassment, a serious setback or a complete catastrophe?

P.M. I want to be very clear about this. The government will continue to get on with its job of running the country, and I'm sure the electorate aren't so fickle as to be swayed by a single, and as I say, as yet entirely uncorroborated story. Thank you.

Reynolds Have you heard from him?

P.M. We're currently liaising with a number of specialists, assisting them in addressing certain telecommunications issues not uncommon to that particular region, and hope to re-establish contact in the very near future.

Kite You mean 'no'.

P.M. Thank you so much everybody. Thank you very much.

> *P.M. walks out of the press conference and into an adjoining office, dragging his tie from his neck and throwing his papers into the corner. Anthea is waiting for him*

Have I actually got any flesh left or did those vultures just pick me down to the bone?

Anthea You'll survive. Thick skin. Brass neck.

P.M. I thought you were visiting the family.

Anthea I've been.

P.M. There and back? Have you grown wings?

Anthea Requisitioned an army helicopter.

P.M. What? Don't you think I'm in enough hot water here already, without you standing over me with a boiling kettle? That's the kind of thing reserved for a national disaster.

Anthea Your point being?

P.M. Very good. I suppose I walked straight into that, didn't I? And how was she, the lovely Penelope?

Anthea Pretty inscrutable, actually.

P.M. Sat next to her at a dinner party once, like talking to the fucking Sphinx. Has he called her?

Anthea She says not. I think she was telling the truth.

P.M. Get a tap on the phone.

Anthea Already done it.

P.M. Numbers?

Anthea Er . . . mobile or landline?

P.M. Number numbers. Opinion polls. Crosses in boxes.

Anthea They've . . . gone south a little. Down four points across the board. On average. Less in some.

P.M. And more in others. Because of the photo?

Anthea Because it was an unforgivable thing to do. Which means he's finished as a politician. And without him in the party . . . (*Nervously.*) What is there to like? That's the vibe we're getting.

Pause.

P.M. Thank you. You can go now.

Anthea Go where?

P.M. Wherever you beautiful young things go after work. Eat. Drink. Smoke. Snort. 'Chill out'.

Anthea Shouldn't we be monitoring the wires? It can only be a matter of time before he makes contact, or we pick him up.

P.M. Ha!

Anthea What's 'ha!'?

P.M. Pick him up? That's hilarious.

Anthea Why? It's not like he's lost in the middle of a rain forest.

P.M. He's in Europe.

Anthea Exactly.

P.M. Oh, you think that's a good thing? Hm? Let me tell you what Europe is – a nightmare. A big effing nightmare. Oh, it's always been a zoo, full of weird and exotic creatures, but at least they were all in their cages, eating their own food, talking their own gobbledygook, shagging their own kind. Then someone thought it

35

would be a good idea to open all the doors and pull the fences down, and now look at it, it's just one big safari park crawling with beasts and monsters. Druggies, pushers, peddlers, chisellers, chancers, hackers, hawkers, scammers –

Anthea Nobel prizewinners, brain surgeons, human beings . . .

P.M. – people traffickers, ivory smugglers, gun-runners, dog-eaters, carjackers, kiddie-fiddlers. Nazis, proto-Nazis, crypto-Nazis, neo-Nazis, born-again Nazis, anarchists, fanatics, fraudsters, gangsters . . . Russians.

Anthea Are you finished?

P.M. Bigamists, kidnappers, triads, little Hitlers, mercenaries, hate-preachers . . . one big Jurassic Park and all the monsters rampaging and slithering and . . . and crapping everywhere – you can't put one foot in front of the other down the Champs Elysées without skidding in the mess, you can't go half a mile down the autobahn without ploughing into some huge festering dung heap. One colossal steaming cesspool, that's what it is, with all the sewage of a continent sloshing about and every turd in a million square miles trying to squeeze through that soil pipe we call the Channel Tunnel. And just me with my finger in the hole, keeping it all out.

Anthea I don't remember reading all that in our manifesto. I thought we were pro-Europe.

P.M. The point is this. It's a netherworld, and he's just fallen through the trap door.

Anthea He might not even be in Europe. Half of Istanbul lies in Asia.

P.M. If he's crossed that bridge there really is no coming back. Iraq? Iran? Syria? The road to Damascus – that's the road to nowhere.

Anthea Who said anything about a road?

P.M. Meaning what? Anthea? Anything you need to share with your father?

Anthea We had a report . . . unconfirmed. That he might have taken a boat. He might be on a boat.

P.M. At sea? Of course he is. He's on a boat. Smith, the naval man. Where else would he be?

SCENE TEN

Magnus at home reading from the copy of The Odyssey *given to him by Anthea.*

Odysseus and the crew on the boat.

Magnus
They sailed from Troy, the battle won.

Odysseus and his fellow countrymen
with no thoughts other than home:
Ithaca – the outstretched arms
of its bay – the love of their wives.
They stole into towns along the shore by night,
took meat and wine and grain
to be shared equally among the men,
no more than they needed
to feed their bellies and slake their thirst.
Then their lord Odysseus ordered the retreat:
'Leave the rest. Everyone, back to the boats.'

Odysseus
But my crew were boggle-eyed
with treats, hungry for trophies and souvenirs,
slaughtered one too many innocent lamb,
made sparks where embers were cooling to ash.

Then an enemy stirred, woke,
leapt from its sleep in the hills,
came raging, incensed, like forest fire
driven by fast dry winds,
chasing towards the coast.

We ran, untied the ropes, skedaddled in the boats,
swung our oars through the waves,
rowed and rowed for the blind horizon
where the night sky sat on the black sea. Rowed
    for days.

Polites

You sent for me.

Odysseus

Any signs of landfall? Any omens?

Polites

No nesting birds to speak of,
but leaves on the surface, and a morning haze,
and two river-dolphins yesterday. We must be close.

Odysseus

How are the supplies?

Polites

Low on water on account of what was spilt
when we pushed off in all that mayhem.
Low on food.

Odysseus

And the men?

Polites

They want to find land soon so they can light a fire –
    cook up a hot meal.
They're grumbling like stray dogs.

Odysseus

When you're prowling from one cove to the next,

when you stink of the world – that's how it feels.
They need to get home. They're turning wild.

Eurylochus
Land! Land ahead, and sand to beach in.

Odysseus
Make for that bay.
We'll take on water,
make a fire for the night, give sacrifice and prayer,
roast the best of the meat.
And send a party inland –
see what people live there – people like us, perhaps –
and if there are breads or crops to be had.
Then we'll sail first thing next day.

Polites
You heard him. Drop the sail. Coast quietly into
the bay.

SCENE ELEVEN

*The Smith family home. Penelope and Magnus are in the
house. The phone is ringing.*

Penelope Leave it.

Magnus But what if it's him?

Penelope He'll leave a message.

Magnus How's that going to look?

A mobile phone rings.

Penelope Leave it.

Magnus I'm leaving it, OK?

The doorbell rings.

Penelope How many of them are there?

Magnus (*looking of the window*) Thirty? Forty? Hard to say with all those cameras and microphones.

Penelope Come away from the window.

Magnus How can I count them without looking? I thought what's-her-face was supposed to be sorting some security out. One hobby-bobby with a torch, he was never going to stop this mob. She must have known it would be like this.

Penelope That's true.

Magnus I could pick them off with my bow and arrow. From the roof. There must be some ancient law of the land that says an Englishman in his castle is entitled to put an arrow through a trespasser's skull. They're well within range.

The phone rings again. And the mobile. And the doorbell.

Penelope (*relenting*) Let them in.

Magnus Are you kidding? They're a pack of hyenas. They'll strip us bare.

Penelope Let them in. They can camp out in the hall. You put the kettle on, I'll go and look for some wine in the cellar.

Magnus You put the kettle on. I'll get the wine – I know where it is.

SCENE TWELVE

The Prime Minister's office. The P.M. is on the phone.

P.M. Put me through to the Admiralty. Thank you. (*Pause.*) Norman, about this map. Yes I've got it, but

what bloody good is it? (*Pause.*) Well, I might have
said a map of the sea but I meant a map of the coast,
obviously. (*Pause.*) What good is a map of the sea, it's
just a square of pale fucking blue with nothing on it.
(*Pause.*) Well it might be very detailed to you lot with
your frigates and submarines but to me . . . why would
I be interested in sandbanks and reefs, I'm looking for a
government minister not a shoal of herring. It's just blue.
You might as well have sent me a map of the sky. You
might as well have sent me a fucking windowpane or a
jar full of water. (*Pause*) Yes. Yes. Exactly. With some
land on it. And some place names. Thank you. Over and
out. (*Puts phone down.*) Anthea?

SCENE THIRTEEN

On land. The next day.

Odysseus
A bright morning and a friendly wind. All prepared?

Polites
All the pots and bags filled and stowed.

Odysseus
Where are the others?

Polites
You sent them inland – they haven't returned yet.

Odysseus
What time did they set out?

Polites
Just before dusk last night.

Odysseus
Which way did they go?

Polites

That steep path by the cliff. See, where those flowers bloom.

Odysseus

You mean the . . . Not those?

Polites

Beautiful, aren't they? And the smell.
I'd swear the scent of them was making me quite light-headed.
I dreamed of when I was a boy, in my father's garden . . .

Eurylochus (*calls out*)

My beautiful leader. My beautiful friends.

Polites

Here they are. Call off the search party.

Odysseus

Bring me a rope from the ship.

Polites

I thought you wanted to sail. Now you want to hunt?

Perimedes

Come here by the flowers. Come and feast with us.

Eurylochus

Odysseus, bliss to you, my king, bliss, my old friend.

Polites

Are they drunk? Have they found wine?

Odysseus

Those are lotus flowers. The fruit and the seed
when taken on the tongue . . . they say
the gates of perception are flung wide and the spirit soars.
But when the feeling dies, the soul enters a chasm.

Fetch the rope.

Perimedes
Odysseus, come taste what we've found.
Honey of all honey. Sugar of all sweetness.

Eurylochus
Old friend, you have landed us in paradise.

Perimedes
Such smoothness enters the mind.
Colours are endless and limitless.

Eurylochus
Ask me what I feel, my beautiful comrade.
I feel a vast, velvet pleasantness.

Perimedes
I feel a smooth purple ecstasy.

Eurylochus
I feel harmony. The golden harmony.

Odysseus
Take nothing from them. Don't even smell their breath.

Eurylochus
The rapture of all mankind uncurls in me.
The gods are in my bloodstream.
All the joy of existence, the rush of life . . .

Perimedes
And the wonder, the wonder . . .
Every nerve in my body vibrates in orgasm . . .
Here it comes again . . .

Odysseus
Tie them and haul them back to the ship.

Perimedes
Ropes? Not ropes. Why ropes, Odysseus?

Odysseus
And search their pockets for those fatal plants.

Eurylochus (*beginning to panic*)
Odysseus, comrade, beautiful friend, don't pain me.
It's all here and it's all free.

Odysseus
Be silent. Pull yourself together.

Eurylochus
Taste it for yourself – the essence of it.
Don't grieve me, Odysseus.
Give me my flower.

Perimedes (*heading towards a tantrum*)
It isn't yours to take away.
You've got your own gods, why can't we worship
the flower,
float in the fever of its pollen for ever?
GIVE ME MY FLOWER.

Odysseus
Throw it on the floor. All of it.

Eurylochus (*beginning to weep*)
You destroyer, you killjoy . . .

Perimedes
You assassin, you executioner . . .
This is TORTURE.

Eurylochus (*sobbing*)
This isn't . . . fair.

Odysseus
Turn out his pockets.

Eurylochus
Those flowers are mine, mine, mine.

He dissolves in tears.

Perimedes
Death to you, Odysseus. You tyrant. You murderer.

The two men are hauled on to the ship protesting and weeping pathetically.

Odysseus (*shouting after them*)
Tie them on deck until they stop jabbering.
And wash your hands in the sea. I want no spores
of that crazy species dusting the air
or spiking the wine or seasoning the food,
or taking root under someone's boot.

I don't want them hungry for drugs.
I want them ravenous for one thing only. Home.
HOME!

SCENE FOURTEEN

The Smith family home. Kite and Reynolds are in the hall, enjoying a meal.

Reynolds Very generous of her to bring us in out of the cold. Very noble.

Kite A bit naive if you ask me. Would you let someone like me in your house, poking around in your wardrobe, making sarky comments about your soft furnishings? Very amateurish, thinking she could buy us off with a cup of tea and a biscuit.

Reynolds It's a bit more than that. This is the best meal I've had in months. And this wine isn't just your supermarket plonk – it's proper vintage. That kid keeps fetching it up from the cellar.

Kite They must be loaded. There's a great story here, I can smell it.

Reynolds Look at this Stilton. Get a good whiff of that.

Penelope appears on the balcony. Cameras begin clicking.

Hold up. Here we go. (*Calling up to her.*) Penelope? Mrs Smith?

Kite Down here, Mrs Smith. Can we have a word?

Reynolds Can we have an interview, Mrs Smith?

Kite Any comment on the photograph? Has he made contact with you, Mrs Smith?

Penelope turns away and goes into her room.

Reynolds Now look what you've done. You've gone and scared her off.

Kite She'll be back. Anyway, we've got people on every gate and cameras on every window. Got a nice one yesterday when she came out of the shower.

Reynolds That's a disgrace. Let's have a look.

Kite shows Reynolds a photograph on his mobile phone.

Kite Colin took it. He's in a sycamore tree about three hundred yards away with a lens like a bazooka.

Reynolds It's a bit blurred.

Kite Yeah, well, couldn't publish it anyway, taste and decency and all that, but nice for the private collection. Bit of a stunner, isn't she?

Reynolds Yeah she's in good nick.

Kite So what are your lot after?

Reynolds Exclusive interview. Daily instalments. From the heart. Backstory, some nice pics, house and garden, composed portrait – elegant but alluring, twin set and fishnets sort of thing, all the bedroom gossip. Oh, and some political whistle-blowing. She might as well dish the dirt, if he's a goner.

46

Kite You don't get this rich and this powerful without being a bastard, there's scandal here if you dig deep enough, that's for definite. How much are you offering?

Reynolds Well, that would be telling, wouldn't it?

Kite Whatever it is we'll double it. This is the jackpot. We're going all out.

Magnus has been hovering in the background listening to their conversation. As he moves towards them he accidentally-on-purpose spills a tray of food over them.

Kite Oi! You clumsy sod.

Magnus Sorry.

Reynolds It's OK, don't worry about it, son. You're Smith's boy, right?

Magnus Yes.

Reynolds Not at school today?

Magnus Couldn't get out of the drive because of you lot.

Kite Which school do you go to? Private, is it?

Magnus Very private.

Reynolds Good answer. Tell him nothing. What about your father though, you must be worried sick, eh? Very upsetting.

Kite Did you see the photograph? Any comment?

Magnus Yes. Kiss my arse, and get that peeping tom out of that tree or he'll get an arrow in his forehead.

Kite So that's not very nice, is it? Obviously a bit of a violent streak running in the family.

Reynolds It's Magnus, isn't it?

Magnus Shove it.

Kite Sure, keep it up, son. The bigger your mouth the better the story. And we'll have another bottle of the red, please, and the dessert menu. When you're ready. No rush, we're not going anywhere.

SCENE FIFTEEN

Odysseus
The wind rose, hauling us forward.
The drugged men wailed,
shivered until their bones rattled.
They puked and went pale. Then sat and stared,
their eyes sinking into their heads
like jewels thrown overboard.

Landfall came quickly. Before we knew it
the boat had run aground on a shelf,
whispered to a halt in soft sand. Land,
but not home. We'd heard the folklore
of that place, rumours of a one-eyed freak
roaming the cliffs. Cyclops – Poseidon's weird son.
We should have steered clear, but the thought of food
and fresh milk took us straight to his cave.

SCENE SIXTEEN

The Prime Minister's office. The P.M. is at his desk. Enter Anthea.

Anthea We've got something.

P.M. Tell me.

Anthea CCTV footage from an abattoir on the coast of Greece.

P.M. He's holed up in a slaughterhouse? I see irony's been putting in a double shift.

48

Anthea There was some kind of fracas and fire there, one of our ships picked it up on a thermal image, then we hacked into their security monitors. This was about an hour ago.

P.M. Get it on the screen.

Anthea It's a single camera. Fixed lens. Not exactly cinemascope.

P.M. Show me.

SCENE SEVENTEEN

In Cyclops' cave.

Perimedes
Has he really only one eye?

Eurylochus
That's what they say.

Perimedes
So why should we fear – he's already half blind.

Eurylochus
What do you say, Polites?

Polites
One eye only, but it's as wide and as deep and as clear
as a barrel of rain. So he'll see us alright, if he's in
    range.

Perimedes
If his eye's so big there can't much room for his ears.
So we can sneak up on him while he looks the other
    way,
and he won't hear a thing! Then . . .

*He mimes the action of slitting a throat. Eurylochus
looks away, disturbed by the idea.*

49

Polites

There's room alright, because his head is as big as
a tree stump.
Now pipe down.

Perimedes

Cave's empty – apart from the smell.
But these buckets aren't, and neither are these stalls.

Eurylochus

Come and feast your eyes on this lot. Cornucopia.

Perimedes

There must be five dozen goats here.

Eurylochus

They're sheep, you idiot. You must be from Athens.

Perimedes

Alright, Mr Son-of-the-Soil. Sheep, goat, what's the
difference?
We'll stuff our faces tonight.

Eurylochus

What's in the buckets?

Perimedes

Milk, is it?

Eurylochus

More like cheese, or whey.

Perimedes

Well whey–hey! It's like he knew we were coming
and laid on a feast.
Let's get everything back to the boats.

Odysseus

We should wait.

Perimedes

Wait for what?

Odysseus
>He might make us welcome here. Give us this food
>>as a gift.

Perimedes
>He's a one-eyed nutter who eats people alive.
>I'm not hanging around to sample his hospitality.

Odysseus
>I SAID WE WILL WAIT.
>We're not savages.
>We're not rampaging from shore to shore
>without cause,
>we're making the long journey home.
>Get your minds above your bellies for a minute.
>Today we'll be civilised.

SCENE EIGHTEEN

The Prime Minister's office.

P.M. I can't make out a damned thing. Twiddle with something, can't you.

Anthea It's on full brightness.

P.M. Well, turn the sound up.

Anthea There's no soundtrack, it's just film.

P.M. Spool it on a bit. I've seen better endoscopies than this.

SCENE NINETEEN

Eurylochus
>What about you?

Perimedes
What about me?

Eurylochus
What's the first thing you'll do when you get home?

Perimedes
Obvious, isn't it?

Eurylochus
Alright, what's the second thing?

Perimedes
I'll probably do it again.

Eurylochus
I've got a little plot of land above the cliff.
It's not much but it feeds me and the family.
It's probably gone to seed by now.
Well, first I'll build the walls back up,
make it all trim and tidy. Get some livestock, build up
    a bit of a flock.
Then, every dusk, I'll say a prayer to Zeus,
and throw a stone in the sea, and swear on that stone
never, ever, ever to set foot on a boat again.
I'm going to plant myself in that field,
and I'm going to take root.

Polites
Something approaches.

Odysseus
Is it him?

Eurylochus
He's . . . he's enormous. Inhuman.

Perimedes
Look at those hands. He'll mangle us.

Eurylochus
We're done for, we're pulp.

Odysseus
Everyone right to the back of the cave,
and total silence.

Cyclops
Yahn,
Than,
Tether,
Mether,
Mimph,
Hither,
Lither,
Danver,
Dic . . .

Eurylochus
What's he saying?

Odysseus
He's counting his ewes into the pen.

Polites
What language is he speaking?

Cyclops
Yahndic,
Tayhndic,
Tetherdic,
Metherdic,
Mimphit,
Yahn-a-mimphit,
Tayhn-a-mimphit,
Tether-a-mimphit,
Mether-a-mimphit . . .

Perimedes
It's babytalk if you ask me. Gobbledygook.

Cyclops (*hearing them*)
WHAT! Grokells! Infesters!

Who squatting in Cyclops' cave?
Who dodging and skulking in shadows in Cyclops'
   cave?

Odysseus (*to Cyclops*)
   Pardon us.
   We're blown off course
   by cruel winds, at the mercy of the sea.
   We fetched up here by chance. We mean
   no harm and hope you might welcome us
   as strangers in a strange land. We offer
   the hand of friendship and our word.
   We are true men, respecters of the gods.

Cyclops
   Cyclops farts in gods' faces. Cyclops pisses on gods'
      feet.

Polites
   He's closing the door – we're trapped like flies in
      a bottle.

Eurylochus
   What's the plan, Odysseus?

Perimedes
   Yes, come on, what's the plan, oh mighty leader?

Odysseus
   Who has wine left in their sacks?
   Pour it all into this one bag.
   Let's see if Cyclops here can handle his drink.

Perimedes
   We should drink it ourselves – at least we'd die happy.

Odysseus (*to Cyclops*)
   Here's a peace offering from the men of Ithaca.

   He throws Cyclops the wine sack.

Cyclops
What Ithaca man name?

Odysseus
Er, Nobody, that's what they call me.
Nobody's my name.

Cyclops
Nobody? Huh, Nobody. Cyclops drink wine. Cyclops
    eat Nobody last.
Cyclops save Nobody for pudding. Ha!

*He begins guzzling the wine, then gurgling and singing
to himself.*

Odysseus
Listen to him – he's a stranger to alcohol.
He doesn't know the boozy fumes of the grape.
Wait till it floods through his veins,
wait till it loosens the knot of his brain.

Cyclops burps and laughs and glugs more of the wine.

See that log in the fire?
See its pointed end – it glows red with heat.

Polites
We'll aim at his heart.

Odysseus
No, into his eye.
We'll blind him, but we need him alive.

Over here, Cyclops. Are you awake? Are you
    wide-eyed?

Cyclops
Who shout Cyclops?
Nobody man. Cyclops hungry for Nobody now.

Odysseus
Here I am, in the shadow.

To his men:
Look how his pupil dilates. Wait till it stretches wide.

To Cyclops:
See me now? Here by the rock. Here's Nobody for you.

Cyclops
GGGGGGGGRRRRRRRNNNAAWWWWWWWW.

Perimedes
He'll smash us to pieces. He's got the jaw of a lion.

Eurylochus
And the teeth of a shark. The gods have deserted us.

Polites
This is doomed, Odysseus.

Cyclops
Cyclops eat now,
chew Nobody's flesh,
bite out Nobody's heart,
tear off Nobody's head . . .

Odysseus
NOW!

The men run forward and drive the burning stake into Cyclops' eye. He lets out an ear-splitting scream.

Odysseus
Drive. Drive. Drive.
Ram it all the way home . . .

Cyclops
NNNNNAAAAAARRGGHHHHHHHH . . .

Odysseus
. . . Heave, heave.

And every one of us gave it our full weight,
hammered that burning stake into his head,

Eurylochus

and when the eyeball burst we were soaked in ink,
and the lens crunched and cracked like splintering ice,

Perimedes

and the lashes and eyebrows flared like burning grass,
and we leaned, and heaved, and jammed it further in,

Polites

until the retina sheared, and the optic nerve
spat and seared and spasmed and fused in the heat.

Perimedes

All the while he screamed into the cave,
roared his pain into the booming, echoing rock,

Eurylochus

so loud that other one-eyed monsters on the island
came to listen. They gathered outside and called,

Polites

'Hey, you in there, what's all the fuss and palaver?
Who's giving you grief?'

Eurylochus

And Cyclops, writhing in pain,
his head in flames, shouted:

Perimedes

'Nobody. Nobody hurts Cyclops.'

Polites

So they shrugged their shoulders and padded off home.

Odysseus

A master-stroke on my part, and it worked.
When we drew out the stake it was like a bung,
like a cork, like a plug – blood spurted and plumed,
but I didn't finish him off, the thick-headed brute. Why?

Polites

He'd rolled a stone across the cave's mouth, blocking
the gap,
a stone so vast that he alone could shift it from the
hole.

Odysseus

And this was the whole point of my ingenious plan.
The flock were cowering away from the noise and
flames.
Twines and twisted willow-strands littered the floor.

Perimedes

Each man lashed himself tight under a fat ram,
and two other rams were tethered alongside
to shield him at the flanks as he dangled and clung on.

Eurylochus

Then they ambled forward, tottered over the stone
floor,
bleated to be let out of the cave for water and pasture,

Polites

and Cyclops, even with a smoking hole instead of
an eye
was still a shepherd at heart, so he rolled away the rock,

Eurylochus

opened the mouth of the cave and counted them out,
stroking their backs as they wandered into the light:

Perimedes

'Mether, tether, mimph, hither, lither, anver, danver . . .'

Polites

The ignorant swine, he released them one at a time,
each big ram with a man slung under its gut.

Odysseus

And I was the last man to escape, suspended beneath

the cockiest ram of the lot, my fingers twisted
into the deep shag of his coat, my feet stirruped
in the swags of elastic skin to the inside of his leg.

SCENE TWENTY

The Prime Minister's office.

Anthea Well?

P.M. It's . . . I don't know. Very vague. Inconclusive.

Anthea We could try to get a better resolution. Enhance
the image.

P.M. To prove what? That our embarrassing renegade
is now causing havoc in the international meat industry?
I suppose it was all halal and now it's been contaminated
by the infidel and his filthy henchman. Walk away.

Anthea It was him. Definitely. We should send someone in.

P.M. To do what? He's gone. Disappeared into the night.

Anthea At least he's still alive.

P.M. It would seem so. And you're rapidly becoming one
of the few people in the world who thinks that's a good
thing. I'm beginning to wonder about you two.

SCENE TWENTY-ONE

Odysseus
    Once on the boat with the men and the flock
    and the buckets of cheese and barrels of milk
    the men goaded the Cyclops with taunts, and he
       hurled rocks
    from the cliff but they only caused ripples
    that pushed us further to sea. The wide open sea.

Magnus (*reading from* The Odyssey)
And they cheered and laughed until light,
when it dawned on them that nothing had changed.
Still lost, still famished-hearted, still years from home.

With their fate now in the hands of the gods
they drifted on wind and current, hoping again,
hoping against hope, praying, looking for land.

He throws the book aside.

Load of old crap.

SCENE TWENTY-TWO

Smith family home. Magnus storms into Penelope's room with a tabloid paper in his hand.

Magnus Have you seen this. Have you? Have you?

Penelope Why aren't you at school?

Magnus Do you think I can show my face with all this stuff in the paper? 'Sordid secrets of Smith's sleazy past'.

Penelope Alliteration.

Magnus What?

Penelope If you're not going to school I'm legally obliged to teach you at home. All those 's' sounds: alliteration.

Magnus Aren't you bothered about this?

Penelope Obviously I'd prefer it not to be happening, but . . .

Magnus Other women. Affairs. Fraud. Guns. Bankruptcy. Some old girlfriend saying he liked to tie her up and put a gag over her mouth.

Penelope Magnus . . .

Magnus Front page, back page, middle page, all over the internet.

Penelope Ignore it.

Magnus It's all there is. That's like saying . . . ignore oxygen. Like saying don't breathe. It's everywhere.

Penelope It's lies. You know that.

Magnus Do I? Looks pretty real in here.

Penelope Lies. All of it. Apart from . . .

Magnus Apart from what?

Penelope We're not bankrupt. But we are, might be . . . hard up. Temporarily.

Magnus How can we be hard up? We live in a mansion. There's a top-of-the range Bentley sitting in the garage. We're the richest people I've ever met. Look around – we're rolling in it.

Penelope We borrowed money from the bank. Against the house. It's not a fortune but . . . I mean we won't starve.

Magnus But what?

Penelope I've spoken to the lawyers. It's complicated. Worst case scenario, we'll lose it, if he doesn't come back.

Magnus Isn't he coming back?

Penelope We need to plan ahead, Magnus. We need to think like him, do what he'd do.

Magnus You mean shag half the women in the country, hock the house, get pissed and slash a woman's throat.

Penelope Be strong and smart is what I mean. And you need to grow up.

Magnus Thank you very much.

Penelope Stop being his boy. Start being his son. Can you do that? For your mother?

Magnus Sibilance.

Penelope Sorry?

Magnus All those 's' sounds: sibilance. Stinking slithering sleazy slime-ball scumbags. Sibilance.

Penelope Leave me the newspaper. If you've finished with it.

Exit Magnus. Penelope sits down to read the paper. Then she goes to the answering machine and replays the message Smith left when he called from the airport.

SCENE TWENTY-THREE

The Prime Minister's office. The P.M. is going through the papers.

P.M. Who's leaking all this fucking stuff?

Anthea Calm down. And you've got a foul mouth – would you speak like that in front of other women?

P.M. You're family.

Anthea Why is that different?

P.M. They've even got a photograph of his wine vault. His fucking wine vault! We brought him into the inner circle for a bit of street cred and there he is with . . . (*Puts his glasses on.*) Is that a 1961 Chateau Latour? Even I haven't got a '61 Latour.

Anthea I suppose you'd prefer it if he had a cellar full of coal and beer barrels?

P.M. I'd prefer it if the gutter press weren't poking around in Lady Penelope's pantry and knicker drawer. Who's letting them in?

Anthea She is.

P.M. What? Why?

Anthea There'll be a reason. She's no mug.

P.M. Tell me about it. I once sat next to her at a dinner party. Like sitting next to . . .

Anthea The Sphinx, wasn't it? The 'fucking' Sphinx.

P.M. Any more sightings or reports?

Anthea Nothing reliable.

P.M. He'd better pray to high heaven that we find him before they do, or the next time we see him he'll have a black bag over his head and somebody standing behind him with a ceremonial sword. Maybe we should say a few prayers ourselves.

Anthea I didn't know you were a religious man?

P.M. I'm not really. Tried it once, didn't seem to make much difference. Your mother's very religious, you know. Came home one day and said she'd found God. I don't think she had, I think she'd found Marks and Spencer's.

SCENE TWENTY-FOUR

Odysseus and his men have landed on the island of Aeaea. Perimedes and Eurylochus are eating a meal on the beach, sitting beside a campfire. Odysseus and Polites are talking in the distance.

Eurylochus
    This is the sweetest food.

Perimedes
    Yes, stag. I feel big when I've eaten stag.

63

Eurylochus

I know what you mean – as if you've eaten its spirit
  as well.
As if the ghost of the stag enters the blood,
making you fearless and proud.
Like you're the king of the woods.

Perimedes

I just meant it's very filling, that's all.

He belches loudly.

Eurylochus

Did you see him kill it? Odysseus?
Brought it down with one throw of the spear – thwack.

Perimedes

Got lucky I reckon.

Eurylochus

Splintered its backbone. I saw him dragging it down
  to the beach,
hauling it on a rope made from creepers and vines.
Then gave us the pick of the meat. Really generous.

Perimedes Are you leaving that rib?

Odysseus

Listen to me, men. I've been up on that crag
surveying the interior, trying to make a plan.
It's mysterious here. The plateau is dense jungle,
crammed with ancient trees that interweave
and link arms. Animal noises came to me,
but no beasts I could name from their voices.
I saw birds with feathers like flames, and plants
that swallowed insects, and lizards more like dragons
with double tongues and black smoking breath.

This is a disorienting island, no question of that.
In truth, it's hard to tell east from west,
or even dawn from dusk. To look for sweet water

64

and fruit we have no choice – we'll have to strike
    inland.

The men groan and protest.

Perimedes
But every time we go inland we come face to face
with some bunch of crazies trying to cut us to shreds,
or some one-eyed retard, or some other nightmare.
Why don't we finish our meal, get back on the boats
    and sail?

Odysseus
That's enough bellyaching.

Eurylochus
At least on the water there's only the weather to
    bother about;
what's a few thunderstorms compared with a flesh-
    eating ogre,
or flowers dosed with brain-addling drugs?

Perimedes
I loved those drugs.

Odysseus
A volunteer to lead a reconnaissance party.

Polites (*resigned to the task*)
That would be me.

Odysseus
Brave Polites. Take these two with you.

Perimedes
Why us? Go yourself if you think it's such a good idea.

Odysseus
And come back to an empty beach
and you rowing into the sunset – no thanks.

I'll watch and listen for signs and signals.
May the gods of good fortune smile on you.

The reconnaissance party make their way through the wooded interior of the island.

Perimedes
Ouch!

Polites
What?

Perimedes
Mosquitoes. I've given up counting the bites.
I've got more bites than skin.

Polites
They can smell the fear. It's fear that attracts them.

Eurylochus
Well, they must be having a feast day with me
and I don't mind admitting it. I'm shitting myself.

Polites
Look, in the clearing. What a magnificent palace.
Only someone of great nobility could live there.

Perimedes
Or great cunning.

A beautiful song drifts through the palace door and out towards them.

Polites
Captivating. Enthralling. Enchanting.

Eurylochus
There's no more wonderful instrument than the
    human voice.
My woman used to sing to me while she was cutting
    my hair.

They listen a while longer.

Polites
It's angelic. Inviting.
Keep your weapons close to hand but no sudden moves.
We don't want a bloodbath.
And mind your manners, there's a lady at home.

*They approach the door. The singing is louder and
more beautiful than ever.*

Circe (*seductively*)
Hello, gentlemen.

Polites
Forgive our intrusion.

Circe What's to forgive? I can sing any time,
but it's not every day a band of men call at my door.
Were you washed ashore?

Polites
We've been blown every which way –
will you excuse our untidy appearance?

Circe
I see only the potential in a man,
I look beyond his wind-tousled hair and his torn
clothes.
But don't loiter in the doorway, gentlemen.
Come in and feel the warmth of the fire.

SCENE TWENTY-SIX

On the beach.

Odysseus
Who is it? Don't hide in the bushes, coward,
step on to the path and make yourself known.

Come out of the undergrowth, or I'll hack you to
pieces.

Enter Athena, helmeted, in modern dress, with a long spear in one hand and an anaconda draped around her neck.

Athena
You'd wave your sword at a goddess, Odysseus?

Odysseus
Goddess? What goddess?

Athena
Avert your gaze, Odysseus.

Odysseus
This is a trick. And blasphemy.
Only Athena wears the golden battle helmet.

Athena
Then avert your eyes from the goddess Athena.

Odysseus
I . . . why would a goddess meet a man on an empty
   beach?

Athena
If Athena is the champion of heroic adventure
and the goddess of courage and skill
what better place and time than this?

Look away from the goddess Athena, Odysseus,
   but listen to her voice.

Odysseus
Silver-eyed Athena, with war in one hand
and cunning and cleverness coiled around her neck.
And such fantastical garments, such fine fabrics,
beyond a mortal man's imaginings.
Forgive me. I put away my sword.

Athena
Do that. Because it isn't a weapon you need, it's
   a flower.

Odysseus
To wear as a buttonhole,
to make this vagrant presentable to the vultures and
    wild dogs?

Athena
There's a rare plant that grows here among grass.
The moly flower. Track it down and pluck it from
    its bed.
You'll know it when you see it. The stem is black,
and its black roots have a tight grip on the earth.
But the flower is white. Vibrant, incandescent white.

That flower will keep you safe,
ward off any devilment or spell that comes your way.

Odysseus
It's a trick. You want to see me poisoned,
killed from the inside by some evil bloom.

Athena
When I could lop off your head with one flick of
    my hand?

Odysseus
Show me where this moly flower grows.

Athena
Find it yourself. Grub it out. Remember, black
at the root and stem, petals incandescent white.

Go, Odysseus. Liberate.

SCENE TWENTY-SEVEN

Circe
Does anyone have an appetite? You must be ravenous.

Eurylochus
What a spread. There's enough here to feed an army.

Polites
This is . . . a very welcome surprise.

Perimedes
I wouldn't say no.

Eurylochus
You've just eaten half a stag.

Perimedes
That was breakfast. It's dinner time now.

Circe
Do be seated. Don't stand on ceremony.

Polites
And just the right number of chairs.
It's as if you were expecting us.

Circe
Never underestimate the foresight of the hostess.

Perimedes
No, don't do that, Polites.
And don't look a gift-horse in the mouth either.

Eurylochus (*tucking in*)
So you keep a bit of a farm, do you?
I noticed the stalls in the walled garden.

Circe
I have animals – it's true.

Eurylochus
I have a few sheep myself at home,
and couple of goats. And a pig.

Circe
Fascinating. Won't you take off your cloak
and be seated, Captain?

Polites
I saw . . . I just thought I . . .
Is that a wolf in the garden?

Circe
Probably. It's the smell of the meat.

Polites
He's enormous.

Circe
A bitch – female. But that's a male. See him –
curled under the magnolia tree. He's a beauty, isn't he?

Polites
That's . . . a lion.

Circe
Captain, you do know your natural history.

Polites
Aren't they aggressive?

Circe
They're my puppies. My kittens.
There's no violence here. Give me your hand –

She places his hand over her heart.

Circe
Can't you feel the calmness, the peace, the delight . . .

Polites (*seduced*)
Forgive me. It's been such a long time.

Circe
Here, slake your thirst, before your men drink the
house dry.

Polites downs a full glass of the wine-potion.

Polites
Absolute nectar. Thank you.

Circe (*to Eurylochus*)
  So you were saying you kept animals
  of the porcine variety.

Eurylochus
  Say what?

Polites
  She's asking if you keep pigs.

Eurylochus
  Oh, right. Just the one.

Circe
  How marvellous. They're such comedic,
  entertaining creatures I always think.

Eurylochus
  Yeah, a big fat porker he was, with a SQUOINK!
  Oh, pardon my manners. Must be the wine.
  Haven't tasted such SQUOINK! SQUOINK!

Perimedes
  You can't hold your booze – you're an embarrassment.
  Ignore him, he's a pig! Not fit to GROINK! GROINK!
    GROINK!

Eurylochus
  Are you taking the SQUOINK! SQUOINK!
  Before you laugh at me you should take a look at
    your nose.
  Sorry, I mean snout.
  SQUOINK! SQUOINK! SQUOINK! SQUOINK!

Perimedes has grown a pig's snout on his face.

Perimedes
  Think that's funny? GROINK! GROINK!
  You should see your hands!
  GROINK! GROINK! GROINK!

Eurylochus looks at his hands, which have turned into trotters.

Eurylochus
SQUOINK! GROINK!
Hey, what's GRUNK! GRUNK! going on.

Perimedes
GRRRRRRRUUUUUOOOOIIIIIINNNNNK
Help! Polites! Help!

Circe
Oh, he's got problems of his own.
He can't help you, can you, Captain?

Polites turns around to find a pig's tail at the base of his spine.

Polites
SSQQQQQQQUUUUUUUEEEEEEEEEEAAAAAAA . . .

Enter Odysseus, who has witnessed the transformations through the window or the open door. The pigs run past him into the yard.

Circe
And here's another handsome warrior – the handsomest
    so far.
And wearing his wedding flower.

Odysseus
What have you done to these men?

Circe
They're having fun.
You're very tense, here in the shoulders
and neck. Why don't you relax?

Odysseus
I've come for my men.

Circe
To take them to the butcher's block?
Are you sure it isn't a woman you're looking for?

Odysseus
What sorcery goes on here? What dark arts?

Circe
Sit down at the table.
Doesn't this delicious-looking food tempt you?

Odysseus
You witch my men into pink ugly beasts
and expect me to dine?

Circe
Here, the sweetest wine ever to touch your lips.
Let it loose on your tongue.
Let it loose in your blood.

Odysseus drains the glass.

Ha! You're a thirsty swine. Now go to the sty with
the rest of the litter.

Odysseus
I won't be eating from any trough.

Circe
What! You'll not resist me. Be a pig, I say. Be a pig.

Odysseus
I hear no squealing or grunts.

Circe
BE A PIG. BE A PIG.

Odysseus
I feel no long floppy ears. I see no sprouting tail.

Circe (*she beats his chest*)
PIG. PIG. PIG.

Odysseus grabs her by the neck, half choking her, and draws his sword.

Odysseus

What sort of hog could handle a weapon like this
    one can?
What name will you give to this beast?

Circe

You . . . Odysseus.
Odysseus here in my house!
Fate predicted you'd come one day,
with your twisting words like a bag of eels.

With your . . . iron strength, your quick tongue, your
    golden face . . .

Suddenly passionate:
I can't tell you how long I've brooded on this.
Other men turn to low, pathetic creatures in my eyes,
but you resist, you resist.

Odysseus

One minute she's sending me to the farmyard –

Circe

We'll make magical love, Odysseus.

Odysseus

– the next she's pulling me under the sheets . . .

Circe

We'll bring our powers together, pool our strength.
Mix with me, Odysseus. Let your limbs tangle with
    mine.
(*Whispers*.) Come with me to my bed, Odysseus,
    come with me, come, come . . .

Odysseus

You'll show me some courtesy.

Unlock my men from your spell,

wave your wand over their heads.
Once every ounce of rind on their backs
is restored to flesh, and they stand upright
and speak with a human voice, then maybe I'll taste
a little of what you spread in front of me.

Circe
Whatever you ask – it's yours.

Odysseus
Then swear – swear on your life
you'll point out the way home.

Circe
I promise, Odysseus. I swear.

Act Two

The Smith home. Penelope's chamber. Penelope is putting on her make-up in a mirror. Enter Magnus.

Magnus The pigs are waiting.

Penelope Thank you, Magnus.

Magnus You're going to tell them to clear out, yes?

Penelope No.

Magnus How can you stand them being here, with their snouts in the trough and their fingers in every drawer?

Penelope Trotters.

Magnus What?

Penelope If they're pigs with snouts, then following the same logic they must have trotters, not fingers. More home education.

Magnus They're vermin. Locusts.

Penelope Now you're just mixing your metaphors. How do I look?

Magnus I caught one of them the other day, the ugly one
. . .

Penelope That doesn't really narrow it down . . .

Magnus The one with the bad teeth, Reynolds . . .

Penelope Kite.

Magnus Going through the bathroom cabinet.

77

Penelope He might have been looking for the dental floss.

Magnus STOP IT.

Pause.

It's like you're just going along with everything. Like you've given in.

Penelope Come here, Magnus.

Magnus No.

Penelope Magnus.

Magnus I said no.

Penelope Then . . . just stand by me while I talk to them, will you. Be at my side.

Penelope and Magnus go out on to a balcony overlooking the main hall of the house, Penelope addresses the journalists beneath her.

Thank you for your patience.

Kite Always got time for you, Mrs Smith.

Reynolds Over here, Mrs Smith. This camera. If the boy could just get a bit closer, maybe put his arm around you. Son, could you just put your arm around your mother . . .

Kite There was a reported sighting last week, any comment from you on that?

Reynolds Don't you deserve better than this? What are London telling you, Mrs Smith?

Penelope They're saying . . . missing presumed dead.

Magnus What?

Penelope As far as the government are concerned, that's his official status.

Kite Is that just wishful thinking on their part?

Reynolds Is he dead, Mrs Smith? In your heart, do you think he's dead?

Penelope I have to face the possibility . . . we have to prepare for the worst. I'll give you my story, his story, the whole thing.

Magnus (*under his breath*) I'm not hearing this.

Reynolds Warts and all?

Penelope Tooth and nail, flesh and blood, body and soul. And believe me, there's plenty to say. In fact I'll write it for you, starting today.

Reynolds There's no need to go to all that trouble. My paper have hired a hotel suite in town . . .

Kite We have a limousine at the gate, Mrs Smith, ready to go somewhere private and relaxing where you can pour your feelings out . . .

Penelope In two weeks' time I'll hand it over.

Kite That's three days before the election.

Penelope To the highest bidder. Sealed auction.

Kite The whole story?

Penelope More story than you'll know what to do with. You can have it all – it's no use to me. So if you'll excuse me, gentlemen, I have work to begin.

The assembled journalists explode into a frenzy of activity, phoning their editors with the news, talking money and exclusives.

Kite (*on the phone*) The whole election could swing on this. It's dynamite. I'm telling you, it's pure dynamite.

Reynolds (*on the phone*) Don't sell me short here, whoever gets this is going to clean up. (*Pause.*) Well, you'd better get on to the accountants then, hadn't you?

Penelope goes back into her chamber and sits down at her dressing table. Magnus follows her in.

Magnus You asked me how you looked?

Penelope I did. And you didn't answer.

Magnus Like a prostitute. Selling yourself to those men. Is that metaphor clear enough? You look like a whore.

SCENE TWO

Odysseus and his crew are aboard ship. Circe's words, echoing in their ears, are guiding them towards their next destination.

Circe
Between and amongst the black poplars.
And past the trees of dying fruit,
stinking things, heavy with rot. Beyond those,
to a shore where leaf-mould and decay
make it difficult to breathe. Leave the boat
and walk to the spit where two rivers
curdle and merge. To one side there's a bluff,
a looming, swaying, overhanging rock . . .

Go, Odysseus, cast off. I'll stand on the cliff,
watching you out of sight.
You'll feel my nails in your back,
taste the blood of my parting kiss.

Odysseus
This way, under the crag.
Eurylochus and Polites, accompany me.
Perimedes, wait here and stand guard.

Perimedes

Don't mind if I do.

Polites

If the dead come here, then may the gods keep me
alive.

The agony and humiliation of old age has nothing
on this.

I'll hold my dying breath, I'll cling to life by my
fingertips.

Eurylochus

The air reeks. The breeze carries a sour stench.

Odysseus

Here in the river sand, help me dig a pit, just as Circe
said.

An elbow's length in each direction and a span deep.

*Speaking into the void, he pours each liquid into the
pit in turn.*

Here's drink for the dead. Succulent honey
blended with milk.

And here's drink for the dead. Sweet wine
from the pick of the vines.

And here's drink for the dead. Pure water
from the mountain stream.

Polites

And now the grain, Odysseus.

Odysseus

And here's the seed of the field, a scatter of barley.
And on my return to Ithaca, I swear to slaughter
the prime bull of the herd in the name of the dead,
and light a bonfire of treasure to you, Tiresias.

Polites

See how the liquid bubbles and stews.

Odysseus
Now the blood.

The men manhandle the two scuffling and bleating sheep towards the pit.

Polites
The ram first.
I'll bare its throat for your sword, Odysseus.

Odysseus
No. Have Eurylochus do it.

Calling into the void again:
And here's rich dark blood for the dead.

Eurylochus produces a knife and cuts the animal's throat. Blood spurts and pours into the pit.

Polites
Now the black ewe. Don't fight it, Eurylochus.
Don't break its neck before the blade takes its life.

Eurylochus slits the throat of the black ewe.

Odysseus (*to the ghosts*)
Rouse. Come gather round this purple pool
which overflows in your name. Be drawn to the blood.

The blood of the black ewe gushes into the pit. The harrowing wails and moans of the dead start up in the distance, coming nearer. For a moment Eurylochus stands to one side, looking at his bloodied hand.

Look – now they flock to me, the dead.
Up out of Hades they come,
the souls of the departed.
Unhappy crowd, sorrowful mob.
Young brides, unmarried boys,
babes who died in the cot,
old men who perished alone,

women with their hearts still bleeding,
battalions of men who died at war,
some still in their battledress,
some still with their shields raised.
Look how they swarm
like bats from a cave.
See how this puddle of blood
attracts them from the grave.
Pitiful, pitiful the massed ranks
of the lost, restless in death.
A million troubled, weightless ghosts.

Eurylochus (*frightened*)
Keep them at bay with your sword.
Swish it through the air.

Polites
No, dip the sword in the blood
and call out Tiresias by name.

*Odysseus dips his sword in the blood-filled pit, and
calls out.*

Odysseus
Tiresias – I offer blood on my blade.

Tiresias
Who disturbs Tiresias?
Who stirs him from his sleep?

Odysseus
I . . . Odysseus.

Tiresias
Odysseus, is it? Come to pick my brains.

Odysseus
Here's fresh blood. Drink as much as you please.

Tiresias
Cruel and cunning, Odysseus. No ghost

can resist the taste of liquid flesh.
No soul can refuse communion with the living wine.

He licks at the blood on the sword, then laps at the pool of blood.

Still warm. Still warm.

Odysseus

The sorceress Circe told us you were our only hope.
One question, Tiresias – will I ever reach home?

Tiresias

Ha! That's what brings you here, is it . . .
slumming it with the bone brigade . . .
I'll tell you this much . . . Poseidon won't rest.
You burnt out his son's eye – now he's hell bent on
 revenge.
But will you reach home? You might . . .
Can you ride out the storm – there's a question.
Will it be muscle or brain that lands you back on
 your own shore?

He enters a vision-state.

I see . . .
I see your house, Odysseus, your wife Penelope
besieged by coarse, rapacious men.
A house of suffering . . . a son in pain . . .

Listen, do you hear her singing, Odysseus,
calling you home, your wife, Penelope,
singing her song into the world, into the wind . . .

Steer for her voice, Odysseus.
Set a course for her face.
The vision . . . the vision fades.

Polites

But another comes forward. Who is it?

Eurylochus
I can't tell – it's nothing more than a shade.

Odysseus
Come out from the grave.

Polites
The gods help poor Odysseus. I know that shape.

Eurylochus
You poor, bedevilled man. My poor, tortured king.

Odysseus
Is it . . .
Is it . . .
. . . Mother . . .

Anticleia
Oh my beautiful boy, still alive.

Odysseus
Mother, why are you here with these shabby ghosts?
These phantoms are no company for your living heart.

Anticleia
Not living, Odysseus. My heart has stopped.

Odysseus
No . . . No . . .

Anticleia
There's no pulse, now. No strength
to take my beautiful boy in my arms.

Odysseus
But how . . .

Anticleia
I died of grief for my son.
For you, Odysseus. I died for you.

Once a woman bears a child
her heart's no longer her own.

When that child is lost,
so is the will to go on.

Grief for the missing is worse
than grief for the dead.

I died of longing, Odysseus.
I died of my love for you.

And your wife, Penelope – she waits.
She waits in Ithaca – dying the same death.

Odysseus
No! This is a fabulous trick.
The gods have twisted me one way then another;
they're out to deceive me – this is their latest illusion.

Anticleia
This is what happens once death has chosen us.

The blood drains. The nerves become numb.

Flesh won't cling to the scaffold of bones.

The heat of life cools to a powdery ash.

The bird of the soul flies from its branch.

Her voice begins to fade.

Odysseus *(calling in to the darkness, sobbing)*
Mother, Mother . . .

He falls to his knees in tears.

Polites
Beleaguered man. Sorrowful king. My heart weeps.
Lean on me, my captain, Odysseus,
I'll bear you back to the ship.
Out of this dire hell. Towards the light.

*As Polites steers Odysseus away, Eurylochus looks
again into the void, blood from the sacrifice still wet*

on his hand. Then Briseis approaches, comes closer,
reaches out with her tongue to lick the blood from
Eurylochus' hand. When he pulls back his hand she
disappears into the darkness.

SCENE THREE

Prime Minister's Question Time in a rowdy House of
Commons. The Leader of the Opposition is addressing
the P.M. across the despatch box. The P.M. sits silently,
having to absorb the jeers of the House and the taunts
of his opposite number.

Speaker Order. Order. ORDER.

Opposition Naturally, Mr Speaker, we lend our voice
of sympathy to the Smith family at the passing of Mrs
Smith senior, and our hearts go out to Penelope her
daughter-in-law and Magnus her grandson, whose
distress and anguish at this time can only be imagined.

Parliament Hear, hear. Hear, hear.

P.M. (*getting to his feet*) Thank you for those heartfelt
condolences . . .

Opposition (*shouting him down*) But be that as it may,
Mr Speaker, be that as it may, as the Leader of Her
Majesty's Opposition it would be a dereliction of duty
not to address the current crisis facing this Prime
Minister, a crisis brought about by the shameful
behaviour of one of his own cabinet members, a member
with a chequered personal history to say the least,
promoted through the ranks with an undue haste which
not only brings the Prime Minister's judgement into
question but typifies the arrogance and belligerence of
his leadership.

87

The House echoes with barracking and shouting from both sides.

Speaker Order! Order!

Opposition Mr Speaker . . .

Speaker ORDER! ORDER!

Opposition Mr Speaker, the country goes to the ballot box in less than two weeks' time, and the opinion polls tell their own story. A party in chaos, a government in meltdown, and a Prime Minister with blood on his hands. What have we heard from him, Mr Speaker? I'll tell you what we've heard from him since that despicable act in Istanbul. Excuses, half-truths, shallow sentences, weasel words and diplomatic double Dutch. Well, I say let his tongue slither and slide all it likes because come election time the right-minded and straight-talking people of Britain will speak, and the country will have its say!

The House erupts.

Speaker ORDER! ORDER! The House will reconvene in one hour's time. The House will reconvene in one hour's time.

SCENE FOUR

The P.M. storms into his private office. Anthea is waiting for him.

P.M. That gloating, jumped-up, parasitical little shit of a shit. Oh, he's full of it isn't he, the false indignation, the holier-than-thou, butter-wouldn't-melt-if-you-shoved-it-right-up-my-arse-with-a-hot-fork look on his smug chinless mush. Fucking . . . public schoolboy little handwank of an arsewipe.

Anthea He went to a comprehensive, didn't he?

P.M. Exactly – he's the worst kind of public schoolboy there is – the kind that didn't go to one.

Anthea It's going to take me a while to unravel that thought.

P.M. Little nosebleed. If he thinks for one second I'm just going to roll over, going to say, yes, yes, you're so right, here, let me give you the keys to the kingdom on a sliver salver, sit on his lap and let him shaft me right up the Thames Estuary as far as the Henley Regatta he's got another thought coming. Am I a quitter?

Anthea No, Father.

P.M. And what's the family motto?

Anthea To remain till the end?

P.M. To stand until last.

Anthea In which case, you might need to sit down.

P.M. What? Tell me.

Anthea The girl in the bar. She's dead.

The P.M. sits down.

During the night.

P.M. There's wailing and howling I suppose.

Anthea You suppose right. And an Islamic fundamentalist group have put a price of a million dollars on Smith's head.

P.M. Of course they have.

Anthea And the Arab League are demanding a statement.

P.M. Effigies on fire yet?

Anthea Effigies burning in Cairo, Damascus, Gaza City, Tehran . . . Mostly of Smith, a couple of you. The Embassy in Tunis hit by petrol bombs, unrest in Karachi, Beirut, Lahore . . .

P.M. I get the picture.

Anthea And a representative from the British Council of Muslims insisting on an audience with you.

P.M. Alright. Where and when?

Anthea Actually he's banging on the front door right now, with a petition in his hand.

P.M. (*going to the window to look*) Looks like he's got all the audience he wants. Cameras everywhere. Who the hell does he think he is, Martin fucking Luther?

   Pause.

Well, that's . . .

Anthea Disastrous? A PR apocalypse?

P.M. (*sitting down, speaking thoughtfully*). Sad, I was going to say. How old was she?

Anthea My age.

P.M. You know, I never even asked her name.

Anthea Briseis.

P.M. Briseis. Contact the father. We'll do all we can. He'll be . . . devastated.

Anthea I'll do that. I'm sorry.

P.M. (*pensively*) Nothing for you to be sorry about, my darling. Nothing in this world.

Anthea So is there a plan? A stand-until-last sort of plan?

P.M. I think . . . I think . . .

Anthea Well?

P.M. Hand me my coat. I'll be back in a couple of hours.

Anthea That's more like it. To the barricades, eh!

P.M. No, my sweetheart, to the club, I think. Quiet drink in front of a real fire. The sound of old men snoring, very calming I always find. Probably best if I slip out the back. We do have a back door here, don't we?

SCENE FIVE

Penelope in her bedroom. She is singing to herself while typing on a keyboard. We see various words from the piece she is writing:

'. . . Childhood sweetheart . . . swept off my feet . . . down on one knee . . . secrets and promises . . . the ghosts of the past . . . the north in his bones . . . passionate nights . . . power like a drug . . . the duty of a wife . . . a mother's love . . .'

In his bedroom Magnus is asleep. The curtain flaps a little. Anthea enters the room. She retrieves the copy of The Odyssey *from where Magnus had thrown it into the corner, opens it on a particular page and props it in his hands. As she leaves Magnus wakes. Finding the book, he begins reading.*

Magnus
  Then when our ship had left the tidal river at its stern
  And forged into wide seas with long high waves . . .'

SCENE SIX

On the ship.

Odysseus
Rest the oars for a moment while I talk.

Polites (*shouts*)
Men, rest the oars.

Perimedes (*under his breath*)
Here comes one of those big speeches.

Odysseus
We're not drifting aimlessly, as some of you think.
We have a direction and a destination, and we're
on course.
We didn't visit the Land of the Dead for no reason
but to hear our destiny from the mouth of Tiresias.

Perimedes (*whispering*)
Great, so we got instructions from a blind man.

Eurylochus
And a dead one at that.

Perimedes
Hey, whoever heard of a visionary who can't see?

Odysseus
It's only three or four short hops
from island to island before we reach our home,
our Ithaca.
But it's a hazardous route . . .

Groans from the crew.

Your lives and my life are intertwined.
There's no unravelling the knot. Your lives
depend on mine – you'd do well to remember that.
Now bring me beeswax, softened in a bowl.

Perimedes
What does he want beeswax for?

Eurylochus
Maybe he's going to polish the deck,
to look clean and . . . shipshape . . . when we pull
into port.

Perimedes
Maybe he's lost the plot.

SCENE SEVEN

*At the Prime Minister's club in London. The P.M. is
sitting in a leather chair, reading* The Times. *He is
approached by Magnus, dressed as a waiter, carrying a
drink on a tray.*

P.M. What's this?

Magnus Your drink.

P.M. I didn't order a drink. Not one of those anyway.
Fetch me a whisky.

Magnus sits down in the chair next to him.

Er . . . either you're having some kind of catastrophic
cardiac event, or I suggest you get back on your feet and
disappear out of my sight.

Magnus Lovely upholstery. A seat of power. I bet some
important arses have sat here over the years.

P.M. I beg your pardon, are you out of your fucking
mind? (*Shouting.*) Steward! Steward!

Magnus The arses of the rich and powerful, shining
thiseather with their over-fed buttocks for hundreds of
years . . .

P.M. Steward!

Magnus Resting their big fat behinds while the little people skivvy and graft. Sipping their whiskies and falling asleep over the *Times'* crossword while others do their dirty work, then when it all goes belly up just flushing it all down the drain and washing their hands with that pricey soap in the gentlemen's lavatory . . .

The Steward arrives and holds Magnus in an armlock.

Steward That's enough. You're coming with me.

P.M. (*realising who he is*) It's alright. Let him go.

Steward The police are on their way.

P.M. I said it's fine. Get him a drink. What do you want to drink?

Magnus You can shove your drink.

P.M. He'll have a lemonade.

Magnus I'll have a lager top and a Jägermeister chaser.

P.M. Get him one of those – whatever it is. And if you're old enough to drink you're old enough to have a mature conversation, so if it won't offend your high-minded ideals I suggest you lower your behind into that chair and lower your voice at the same time.

Magnus sits.

Well, you're a chip off the old block, striding in here as bold as brass. Magnus, isn't it?

Magnus Don't know what it says about your security, when someone in a fancy dress costume can wangle his way into the corridors of power and get this close to the Prime Minister.

P.M. Like I said, a chip off the old block.

Magnus Where is he?

P.M. Listen, Magnus . . .

Magnus Government ministers don't just vanish into thin air.

P.M. It's a very sensitive matter.

Magnus Don't tell me it's sensitive. He's my dad. How sensitive do you think that is? Imagine if it was your own father, or your son, or your daughter – I bet the wheels of international diplomacy might be turning a bit quicker if that was the case.

P.M. In fact I rarely saw my own father. In those days . . .

Magnus Oh save me the boarding-school sob story. He's my dad, and I don't know if he's alive or dead.

Pause.

P.M. The girl in the bar. She passed away this morning.

Magnus I didn't know that.

P.M. Complications following surgery. Briseis. She was called Briseis. And now . . . half the world baying for blood, an eye for an eye, a tooth for a tooth. Like I said, it's sensitive.

Magnus Why can't you just be honest with us?

P.M. Because in all honesty – look at me, Magnus, when I say this, because I need you to believe me – with hand on heart, and as much as it embarrasses me and is painful to you – we haven't a clue. Not a notion. He was in an abattoir, he was on a boat, he was in a cemetery, he was in Teletubbyland, he was at the North Pole making Christmas presents with Santa's little helpers . . . a million rumours, zero facts.

Magnus What about the Americans? I heard once that if you put a newspaper on the ground anywhere on the earth the Yanks can read it from space with one of their spy satellites.

P.M. I'm sure they can look so far down someone's oesophagus they can tell what they had for breakfast. But your father . . . he's bad news as far as they're concerned. Not a brush they'd like to be tarred with.

Magnus Which is why you've dumped him as well, right?

P.M. Your father's in a lot of trouble, Magnus. I'm sure he means the world to you – I respect your loyalty. And we're doing everything we can. But he's one man, and whatever you think of the people who park their fundaments in these chairs, which are pretty fucking uncomfortable by the way, they have bigger and wider and deeper concerns than just him.

The Steward brings the drink.

Magnus Not thirsty now.

P.M. Here.

Magnus What?

P.M. My phone number.

Magnus So we can be text buddies.

P.M. Only my daughter and somebody with his finger on a big red button that says nuclear bomb on it has that number.

Magnus So why give it to me?

P.M. To ask for news, and to get a straight answer.

Magnus A straight answer from a politician?

P.M. Person to person. Man to man.

The P.M. offers his hand, but Magnus won't shake it.

How are you getting home?

Magnus Don't know.

P.M. How did you get to London?

Magnus Thumbed it.

P.M. Hmm. I think we can do a little better than that.

SCENE EIGHT

*Penelope typing. The downdraught from a helicopter
blows the curtains into the house and sweeps the pile of
papers from her desk all over the room. Magnus walks
through without speaking, wearing a pair of aviator
shades. Penelope watches him, collects the pages, then
begins typing again.*

SCENE NINE

On the ship.

Eurylochus
  Hey, feel that?

Perimedes
  What?

Eurylochus
  The breeze.

Perimedes
  There isn't any. The sail's gone limp.
  Hanging like a veil. There isn't a breath of air.

Eurylochus
  That's right. That's what I mean.

Polites
  Odysseus? Odysseus?

A faint singing begins in the faraway distance, then fades.

Odysseus

There isn't much time.

Polites

Much time for what?

Odysseus

Men, we're making good headway,
but the Island of the Sirens looms close.

On pain of death, don't let their songs
enter your head. Here's the beeswax –
I've kneaded it all afternoon in the sun.
Here, every one of you, take a gobbet,
and when I give the signal
push it deep in your lugs. Good.

Now get the strongest rope on board
and lash me tightly to the mast . . .
Bind me in coils of rope.

Polites

Sir, we wouldn't dream of roping you like a wild
horse . . .

Odysseus

And then row and row and row.
Dig into the waves as if you were drunk
and digging for gold. No – tunnelling out of a grave,
as if you were buried alive.
And whatever I say, however much I scream
or threaten or plead – ignore every word.

Perimedes

If it's so dangerous how come he doesn't bung his
own ears?

Eurylochus

What doesn't kill you makes you stronger –
maybe he's trying to build up his strength.

Perimedes

And maybe he's just showing off.
The only man to have heard the Sirens and lived –
one more claim to fame, one more feather in his cap.

Polites

But sir . . .

Odysseus

Do it NOW.

They lash him to the mast.

*A silence descends. The noise of the men and the
sound of the waves gradually disappear. The song of
the Sirens enters Odysseus' head. When the Sirens are
seen, perhaps through a veil or gauze, they are
Penelope, Circe, Briseis and Anthea.*

Sirens

Here where the fires burn . . .
Here where the stars glow . . .
Here where the fruits grow . . .
Here where the heart turns . . .
                Come, Odysseus. Odysseus, come . . .

Odysseus (*moaning*)

This is witchery . . . but pleasant. Soothing.

Sirens

Here where the fires glow . . .
Here where the stars turn . . .
Here where the fruits burn . . .
Here where the heart grows . . .
                Come, Odysseus. Odysseus, come . . .

Odysseus

This music touches me. It has fingers and hands.
I feel its breath. I feel its mouth. Oh . . .

Sirens

Here where the fires turn . . .
Here where the stars grow . . .
Here where the fruits glow . . .
Here where the heart burns . . .
       Come, Odysseus. Odysseus, come . . .

Odysseus

Men, put down your work and untie me.
Listen, listen to the pull of it, the pull of it . . .

Sirens

Here where the fires grow . . .

Odysseus

. . . fires grow . . .

Sirens

Here where the stars burn . . .
Here where the fruits turn . . .

Odysseus

. . . where the . . . where the . . .

Sirens

Here where the heart glows . . .

Odysseus

. . . where the heart glows . . .

Sirens *and* **Odysseus**

       Come, Odysseus. Odysseus, come . . .

Odysseus

Sail closer to the shore – that's an order.

Men, angels are calling us – don't ignore them.

All my treasures are yours if you take me closer.

Untie me, I'll stab any man who disobeys me.

Eurylochus, friend, slit these ropes with a blade.

Men – a woman for every one of us – they promise us.

Polites, I command you to sail towards that chorus.

Untie me now. Now. Untie me, you bastard scum.

Zeus, hear me. I'll sacrifice everything in your name.
All my flocks and herds, all my land and estates . . .
All my servants . . . these men . . . take them . . .
(*Desperate.*) Penelope . . . Penelope . . . Penelope . . .

*He wails and moans as the ship passes the island and
the music dies away in the distance.*

SCENE TEN

The Prime Minister's office.

P.M. (*on phone*) Thank you, Norman. Always a
pleasure. (*Pause.*) Yes, indeed, it may well be the last
time we speak, as you say, because unlike you chaps in
the Ministry with your jobs for life and your ironclad
superannuated index-linked triple-locked gold-plated
pensions, some of us are at the mercy of the electorate,
and have to be seen to be doing a good job or we're out
on our tushis. But if I am still here next month then let's
talk again about a career move for you – there's a big
ambassadorial opportunity coming up in . . . no, not
Washington, Norman, in Yemen, I hear, and with your
qualifications . . . Norman? Over and out.

Enter Anthea.

Where have you been?

Anthea Choir practice.

P.M. Singing – in the midst of all this? Isn't that a case of fiddling while Rome's burning? Or rearranging the deckchairs on the Titanic?

Anthea It's food for the soul.

P.M. Well this might spoil your appetite a little. Look.

The P.M. unrolls a large sheet of paper on the table.

Anthea Opinion polls?

P.M. No, a different kind of nightmare. Weather forecast for the eastern Med for the next twenty-four hours. Norman from the Admiralty couriered it over. Likes his maps, Norman, and at least there's some fucking countries on this one.

Anthea It's like a target – that bull's eye in the middle looks a bit angry.

P.M. Worst weather event in twenty years for this time of year. A perfect storm of winds, tides, barometric something or other, and tracking right the way along that coastline. In short, you wouldn't want to be out there in a boat.

Pause.

His boy was here. Magnus.

Anthea So I heard.

P.M. He's got some bollocks, I'll give him that. Anyway, I told him everything.

Anthea But you don't know anything.

P.M. Exactly. But I think he needed to hear it. I think he needed to look me in the face.

Anthea Maybe you needed to look him in the face as well.

P.M. When he was leaving he asked me this strange question. He said, 'Are you Zeus?' What do you think that meant?

Anthea Er . . . no idea.

P.M. 'Are you Zeus? You're Zeus, right?' Probably street slang.

Anthea Yes, probably.

P.M. Rhetorical. Must mean . . . you're the boss. You're in charge.

Anthea That'll be it.

P.M. You're the man, right. The daddy-o.

Anthea Please.

P.M. You're the number one, the head honcho around here.

Anthea Alright.

Zeus The feller with the . . . umbrella.

Anthea What? That's not a thing. That's not even a thing.

P.M. The Big Zee.

SCENE ELEVEN

Magnus reading from The Odyssey. *As he reads we see Odysseus and his men being shipwrecked and falling into the sea.*

Magnus
No sooner did they cast off, no sooner did they
round the point, when black clouds circled and
swarmed,

gathered over the boat like black smoke,
and the air grew thick and tight, full of pent-up rage,
until the stretched bag of the sky exploded in white fire,
thunderbolt after thunderbolt setting the ocean alight.

It didn't take long. The end was quick. The mast
broke like a twig. The keel snapped. The hull
fragmented into kindling and smithereens.
Every man was pitched into the churning swell –
each face went past, gulping for breath, reaching
for a hand or rope or beam or spar or hope.
Arms thrashed, throats burned with salt, mouths
gulped down sea, breathed the sea until lungs
were leaden weights, till the heart was in flood.
And whenever the sky spat with lightning
the sea fought back, the waves reloading
after every volley and crack, summoning its strength
to lash out at the planets and stars, to punch the moon,
white water erupting in vast volcanic plumes
then crashing down into itself. Then waves parted,
and cracks opened as deep as the sea bed, that place
where blind fish live among colourless flowers
and the bones of whales and the teeth of sailors
lie among rocks, so just for a moment those men
saw the floor of the world before the sea slammed shut.

Heads rose and sank, rose and sank, then rose no more.
At dawn, floating debris littered the flat calm.
A packing crate. A leather pouch. A wooden bowl.
A plank. An apple. A glove. A shoe.
Cargo drifted as far as distant beaches and shores.

SCENE TWELVE

*A beach at sunrise. Sea birds and the sound of shallow
waves. Smith is face down in the shingle, half naked.*

He rouses, vomits sea water, then crouches down on the shore, coughing and shivering.

Enter Anthea.

Anthea Passport, please.

Smith (*spinning round*) Is it . . . Anthea?

Anthea You look like you've seen a ghost. Here, take my coat. That's a nasty cut. Someone needs to take a look at that.

Smith Where are the others?

Anthea It was a terrible storm. The worst.

Smith I was in the water for hours.

Anthea Days, in fact.

Smith We were heading north.

Anthea You were going every which way.

Smith How did you find me?

Anthea Intelligence.

Smith Intelligence? Intelligence? So why didn't you come sooner? How come you didn't just fish me out?

Anthea I didn't say Intelligence. I said intelligence.

Smith Don't play Little Miss Enigmatic with me. Better I drowned – was that it? Because that's what my intelligence is telling me.

Anthea You were off the radar. Missing presumed dead. There's a monumental mason somewhere carving a memorial stone with your name on it, so be glad you're alive and be glad I'm here.

Smith And where is 'here'?

Anthea You don't know where you are?

Smith No idea. Tunisia. Corsica.

Anthea Getting warmer.

Smith Malta.

Anthea Colder again.

Smith Acapulco. The Falkland Islands. Katmandu.
Atlantis . . .

Anthea Smell the air, Smith.

Smith Smell it yourself.

Anthea Breathe it in. Right to the pit of your lungs.
Taste it on your tongue. Don't you recognise the tang
and the scent?

Smith I don't know. Flowers or blossom of some kind.
Juniper?

Anthea Juniper? Maybe. Or cypress and balsam and
olive. Pines – that fragrance that drifts off the pine trees
in early morning, rolls down the hillsides, mixing with
the salt in the breeze, and a jasmine and myrtle in the air
as well, that cocktail of aromas . . . a Greek island, in
the Ionian maybe, is that what your nostrils are saying . . .

Smith This is very cruel.

Anthea I think your senses need a little retuning.
Juniper? Vinegar more like, from these chip wrappers on
the beach. Or saturated fats from the doughnut stall in
the car park and the scented wet-wipes in the litter bin,
or fumes from the oil refinery round the headland.

Smith So I don't know my flowers.

Anthea Juniper? Rapeseed flower at best, mingled with
a whiff of the offshore sewage outlet and the carbon

monoxide from the ferry terminal and the exhaust clouds from the motorway in the next valley and the slurry from the superfarm and the pong of the local landfill site a mile downwind, then throw in the stench of a few hundred politicians all sweating on the outcome of next week's general election to decide who rules over this green and pleasant land, and you're much closer to the mark. Welcome home, Minister.

Smith England?

Anthea We prefer 'Britain' as a term, and where you're appealing to the right-of-centre you can stick the word 'Great' in front of it.

Smith scoops up a handful of sand and lets it run through his fingers.

Smith Take me home.

Anthea I can't do that.

Smith You can do it and you can do it *now*.

Anthea Listen to me, half the world is out looking for you and they're not throwing a welcome party. Under international law we're duty bound –

Smith I'm going home.

Anthea – to hand you back to Turkish jurisdiction . . .

Smith Not happening.

Anthea Or . . . and I didn't say this, we can find a safe house, lie low for a while, work out some kind of identity transition . . .

Smith I'M GOING HOME.

Anthea YOU'LL BE RIPPED TO SHREDS, IN EVERY WAY YOU CAN THINK OF. You won't get within five miles of the place.

Smith I'd rather get back in that water than be spirited away to some nothing life in some nowhere land. And you can either help me or you can get out of my way. I'm going back to my wife and my son.

Anthea Alright, alright. Actually. . .

Smith What?

Anthea I thought that's what you'd say. So . . . here. Get changed – I won't look.

Anthea hands Smith a bag. He tips out the contents on the beach. Tatty clothes, glasses, a wig etc. Smith holds up a coat, which is old and creased and threadbare.

Smith Return home in the stinking rags of some old dosser. You sure this wasn't your father's idea?

Anthea There's something else.

Smith What?

Anthea I shouldn't be the one to tell you this. While you were gone. Your mother. She passed away.

Smith Yes. I knew that. I know.

Anthea How?

Smith I don't know. Sensed it. I felt her go.

Anthea I'm sorry.

Smith Get me home.

Smith begins to change into his disguise. Anthea pulls out her phone.

Anthea Magnus? It's Anthea. How are things up there?

Magnus The same.

Anthea How are you getting on with that book I gave you?

Magnus It's depressing. Everyone drowns. You're a sicko for even giving it me.

Anthea Did you finish it?

Magnus Not really. What's the point?

Anthea There's every point. The next bit's very strong, very compelling.

Magnus I'll probably wait till the film comes out.

Anthea Oh, books are always better. They get deep down, under the surface. Improve the mind. Very instructive.

SCENE THIRTEEN

The Smith family home, Cumbria. Penelope is reading the last page of her story. After signing it, she adds the page to the rest of the pile and puts the manuscript into an envelope. At the same time, reporters are gathering in the hall. Anthea is also present, as is Smith, but heavily disguised with a beard and glasses. Kite is presenting a television bulletin.

Kite (*to camera*) There's growing excitement here in Cumbria for what some people are describing as the biggest media event of the year, an occasion which is currently overshadowing the general election itself in terms of news coverage and column inches, and might well have a bearing on the future of this country. In a few minutes' time we're expecting Penelope Smith to stand on that balcony and hand over her story to the highest bidder, a story which, if rumours are to believed, will be a no-holds-barred personal testimony with insights into the darkest corners of our current government. Bated breath here: in all my days as a journalist I can't quite remember anything like it, a heady brew of high-ranking politics, Hollywood-style drama, human tragedy and kiss-and-tell gossip. I can't wait. Back to you in the studio.

Reynolds Very good, very smooth. Yesterday a grizzled old hack, today an all-action television news presenter.

Kite Yeah, well, I've been in on this since the beginning so I wasn't going to let some jumped-up media studies student with her blouse unbuttoned to her belly button come waltzing in and steal the limelight.

Reynolds I always thought you had more of a face for radio myself.

Kite If I land this catch I'll be able to have any face I want. I've always fancied a few nips and tucks around the eyes and mouth – don't want to end up with one of those hangdog expressions that most knackered old journos get in the end – you know the look I'm on about, don't you, Reynolds?

Enter Penelope.

Here we go.

Reynolds You lot are going down.

Kite We're so not going down. This time next week you'll be asking me for a job. And I'll be telling you to suck my dick.

Reynolds Then the doctor will be saying, 'Wake up, Mr Kite, you've been in delusional fantasy brought on by a traumatic blow to your career prospects and a subsequent ego meltdown. Now let's get this bed-pan emptied. By the way, didn't you use to be on the telly?'

Penelope Thank you for your patience. In handing over these pages, I'm acknowledging the reality of the situation:

that my husband won't be returning home, and we have to move on.

Reynolds (*under his breath*) Get on with it.

Penelope Auctioning a life story to the press might appear an unseemly or sordid decision . . .

Kite Come on, love, it's not the Queen's Speech . . .

Magnus Why don't you shut your ugly mouth?

Penelope But I have to think about the future, especially my son's future.

Kite There you go, son, Mummy's always going to look after you.

Penelope So thank you all for your offers, I can now announce . . .

Smith Could I ask a question, please?

Kite Oh for God's sake, just when we were getting to the money shot?

Reynolds Who's this silly old fart?

Smith From the local *Gazette and Journal*.

There are hoots of derision from the assembled press pack.

Er . . . if the auction is still open . . . and I haven't heard the hammer go down . . .

Kite This is an international media event, not Windermere cattle market.

Magnus Windermere doesn't have a cattle market.

Smith Then I'd like to put my own offer in. If you could pass this forward to the lady, please.

Reynolds What's in the envelope – five shillings and ninepence? We've gone decimal you know – 1971 – probably hasn't filtered through up here yet.

Kite Five shillings and ninepence is a lot of money in these parts. I went into one of those pound shops in Ullswater the other day – I bought a house!

Smith That's my bid. So go ahead. Open it up.

Kite Go on, open it. Let's all have a laugh.

Reynolds (*focusing his camera*) Hang on, I don't want to miss this.

Penelope opens the envelope and pulls out her husband's wedding ring.

Kite Hey, you're a fast worker. Popping the question. Talk about bad timing.

Reynolds Is that what you're offering – your hand in marriage?

Kite No disrespect, pal, but I think she's out of your league.

Reynolds Come on, get this prankster out of here and let's cut to the chase.

Smith Well?

Penelope What do you mean by this?

Smith It's your husband's wedding ring.

Penelope I know what it is.

Smith From your husband's hand.

Penelope From the hand of a murderer, then? From the hand that murdered?

Smith Your husband didn't kill anyone.

Penelope And how can he prove that?

Smith He . . . can't.

McGill I can.

McGill steps forward from the back of the room, from where he has been watching proceedings.

Kite This is codswallop. And who the hell are you?

McGill I was in there. In the bar. It was chaos. Fists. Chairs. Knives.

Reynolds She was bottled.

McGill Some idiot smashed one and started waving it around. I ripped it off him. The girl was standing behind me. I felt it . . . going in . . . can still feel it, hear the noise . . .

Kite And how much are they paying you to say that? Do you think we're morons? Not you in the photograph, is it, bottle in his fist, ring on his finger, mad look in his eyes. Eh?

McGill That was Smith. But he wasn't pushing it in. He was pulling it out. This was the hand that killed her. Mine.

There is another, shorter pause before bedlam breaks out. Penelope runs from the hall towards her room. McGill is surrounded by the press. Anthea quietly slips Penelope's testimony into her bag and replaces it with another version.

Magnus and his father stand face to face in silent recognition then share and embrace, before Smith races up the stairs behind Penelope.

Magnus Just like in the book, eh?

Anthea I know, amazing parallel.

Magnus Who are you?

Anthea I'm Anthea, you know that.

Magnus I'm not stupid, and I'm good at anagrams, 'Anthea'.

Anthea I'm the Prime Minister's daughter – that's what it says in *Who's Who*, anyway, so it must be true. Don't forget to feed the animals.

Magnus picks up Penelope's manuscript and starts tearing it into little pieces and throwing it from the balcony like confetti. The journalists scurry around, fighting over fragments of the text.

Kite What's all this gibberish?

Reynolds Looks like Greek. I can't read a bloody word of it.

SCENE FOURTEEN

Penelope and Smith's bedroom. Penelope has gone inside and locked the door. Smith is outside knocking, quietly at first, then with more force.

Smith Penelope. Penelope open the door. Penny, please. PENELOPE.

He barges the door open with his shoulder and enters the room.

Penelope How dare you.

Smith The door was locked.

Penelope This room is private.

Smith It's me. It's me, Penelope. Look.

He rips away his disguise.

I've come home.

Penelope (*furious*) Did you think I didn't know? Do you think I'm utterly stupid?

Smith Everyone else seemed pretty convinced.

Penelope Nobody else has lived with you for twenty years. Do you think a wife wouldn't recognise a husband . . . As soon as you opened your mouth . . . you might as well have hung a sign round your neck.

Smith So why didn't you say something? Acknowledge me?

Penelope Oh yes, it's always about you. Everything in this whole wide world is just for you and for your benefit. I suppose you're expecting a prize for best fancy dress as well, are you? Couldn't just call your wife first, that would have been too easy, way too easy . . .

Smith They said the phones were bugged and I wouldn't get anywhere near you . . .

Penelope You know something? It wasn't the eyes that gave you away, under those pathetic glasses. Or the crappy clothes or embarrassing country bumpkin accent or the bad wig and the false beard – and by the way if that's the best the Home Office can do then they need a new costume department, and God help us if we ever need to go into some kind of witness protection scheme, which seems highly likely after this little escapade . . .

Smith Penelope.

Penelope It wasn't even the mouth, uttering its little lies, or the teeth or the hands. Do you know what it was? Do you?

Smith So tell me what it was.

Penelope The great drama of it all. The big homecoming scene.

Smith Meaning what?

Penelope You couldn't have asked for a better theatre, a bigger stage. Journalists, police, cameras, microphones, helicopters buzzing around overhead, the whole country settling down for the big event – all it needed was a star performance, someone to come striding in and steal the show. Then right on cue– ta-dah! That's how I knew. Because it was *so you*.

Smith They insisted it was the only way.

Penelope Well, of course they did. It's the greatest party political broadcast in history, with you in the leading role – I bet they really had to twist your arm, must have been excruciating.

Smith You were the one who organised the conference, selling your story to those vultures. Whose idea was that?

Penelope What choice did I have?

Smith Yes or no – that was the choice – and you chose yes.

Penelope I was skint. Scared. On my own. I thought if I could keep them interested then I could keep the story alive, keep you alive. I thought . . . if I can keep spinning it out . . .

Smith You were writing my obituary.

Penelope I THOUGHT YOU WERE DEAD.

Smith I THOUGHT I WAS DEAD TOO.

Pause.

I kept wondering . . . is this hell. Is this damnation? What did I do wrong? I did not kill that girl.

Penelope I know that. I've never believed otherwise.

Smith Thank you. Thank you for saying so.

Penelope But you took the blame.

Smith He was terrified. Said if we made it home he'd come clean. Hold up his hand.

Penelope You're so very loyal.

Smith What's that supposed to mean?

Penelope The papers have been having a field day. Photographs. Gossip. Old flames. Affairs.

Smith If you believed that for one second you wouldn't be here now.

Penelope I'd be here alright, and you'd be in a bedsit in Keswick crying down the phone – is that clear?

Smith What about you, here on your own with a house full of men?

Penelope Don't you dare. Not for one second. I am loyalty herself. I am constancy. I am faith. Do you hear?

Smith You are beautiful.

Penelope You are . . .

Smith Tell me. Tell me.

Penelope Very late.

Smith But I'm here.

Penelope A bad timekeeper.

Smith I'll work on my punctuality.

Penelope You'll work on more than that.

Smith Give me a list.

Penelope Being a father. Birthdays.

Smith A deal.

Penelope Priorities. Responsibilities.

Smith I promise.

Penelope Less . . .

Smith I'm listening.

Penelope That person you are out there. The swaggering, cocky man of the world, the walking soundbite . . . leave him at the door.

Smith I know what's important. I want to begin again. Clean slate.

Penelope Perfect. So let's start right now.

Smith Let me touch your face.

Penelope This house needs sorting out.

Smith Sorry? You're talking about decorating?

Penelope Not decorating. Complete refurbishment. It needs gutting and stripping, then we start from scratch. Beginning with this bedroom.

Smith What?

Penelope This cheap crap – it's falling to bits. It's all coming out.

Smith It most definitely isn't.

Penelope Every last nail and splinter. Including that bed.

Smith No.

Penelope It goes. Get rid of it.

Smith (*exploding*) I built that bed with my own hands. Drew the plans, felled the tree, cut the wood, fitted the joints, sanded the grain, carved the headboards. Solid oak that bed, you couldn't shift it even if you wanted to –

you'd have to knock down half the house to get that bed out of here. I built that bed for us. For ever, so it stays put. I'm sorry, alright, so incredibly sorry for everything I've put you through and you've every right to be angry, furious . . . distant. But my world collapsed out there, descended into a nightmare that I can't even begin to describe or explain or understand, and to get back here to this house and to stand with you in this room I have walked and crawled and talked and scrapped and stolen and swum my way through places I didn't even know existed, I've got the dirt from half a continent under my nails and in my hair and half of the world's oceans in my lungs. And this bed . . . this bed was my boat. This was what I sailed in, clung on to, got pitched out of then clambered back into. This bed was my ship and this ring was my compass, my one bearing, my only direction, this ring with your inscription, 'From Penelope, your Ithaca'. That bed and this ring. This is where I live, and this is who I am.

Penelope (*tearfully*) I needed to hear you say it.

Smith Don't shut me out, Penelope. Let me come home.

She leads him towards the bed.

SCENE FIFTEEN

The Prime Minister's office. Enter P.M.

P.M. Anthea. Anthea!

Anthea appears from behind a bookcase, her clothes somewhat dishevelled.

Oh I do beg your pardon.

Anthea It's fine. Just getting ready for the press conference.

P.M. Yes, let's look our sparkling best – not only do we outflank the opposition, we outdress them as well. There's salt in the wound. The numbers?

Anthea Up. And still rising.

P.M. God, I love winning. I love it so much, you know. It's better than anything. Better than sex.

Anthea Oh please.

P.M. I'm speaking figuratively of course, though in this case it happens to be true.

Anthea Probably best not use that turn of phrase in front of my mother, though.

P.M. Sad to report that, with one of those ironic expressions on her face, she'd probably agree with me.

Anthea I'm so enjoying this conversation.

P.M. Yes, one of those expressions. Precisely. Must be in the DNA.

Anthea Did you watch it on the television?

P.M. I certainly did, once I'd got some ten-year-old from the post room to show me how to switch the fucking thing on. Hell of a bun fight. All went to plan, wouldn't you say?

Anthea I would.

P.M. 'Exonerated'. That's the word they're all using. Got a lovely ring to it: 'exonerated'.

Anthea Lovely.

P.M. Exonerated. Exonerated. Exonerated.

Anthea Very nice.

P.M. Yes. Went like a dream. I never doubted it in actual fact, just a question of holding my nerve, keeping a cool head.

Anthea Of course.

P.M. Plenty of people saying I'd backed the wrong horse with Smith, but I just had this feeling . . . his sort, fall in a septic tank then come up smelling of honeysuckle. I know the type, you see. I had this instinct, this inkling . . .

Anthea You've always been a good judge of character.

P.M. It's what gives me my edge I think. I'll develop that theme in the memoirs – make a note of it, will you. Right, time to ram home the advantage. Is this an appropriate tie?

Anthea Perfect.

P.M. That's what I thought. God, I love winning. Am I the dog's bollocks, or what?

Anthea Oh yes, you're the God of Gods, the Father of the Skies.

P.M. Well now, even I would have to say that comparison is a little far-fetched, but if it's how I look in your eyes, my little cherub, then who am I to disappoint you. OK, stand aside for the Man Who Can. Make way . . . for the Jägermeister.

Exit P.M.

Anthea You can come out now. The coast is clear.

Enter Soli from behind the bookcase.

Soli That was close.

Anthea Not quite close enough if you ask me. But we've still got a few minutes.

Soli You still haven't answered my question.

Anthea There'll be lots of time for talking later.

Soli But seriously. Were you tracking us all the way or did you just pick us up that day?

Anthea Well, I'd love to tell you but you just don't have that level of security clearance, Soli, although I'm sure you could, you know, worm it out me. If I was . . . pressed . . .

Soli But Smith first, then me?

Anthea Business before pleasure, you told me that.

Soli I suppose I did. So . . . shouldn't I be debriefed?

Anthea I think that's exactly what should happen.

Soli And I need a bath or a shower. I'm filthy.

Anthea It just keeps getting better and better.

SCENE SIXTEEN

Cameras flash around a table crowded with microphones. The implication is that this is the P.M.'s press conference we are about to witness. It isn't.

Fenton (*striding to the table and sitting down*) I'm gonna keep this short and sweet. Not like those other politicians. Droning on. Anyways, what I saw out there, no man should see. And that's on our doorstep, right. That's twenny miles away across the English Channel, banging to come in. Well, not on my watch. It's late in the day, but for those reasons I'll be standing for Parliament. That's right, sticking up for the little people, those that are British and proud. And I'm launching a new party. So if you like what you hear, come and join us. We're called, United Kingdom One Country.

   Fenton unravels a Union flag which hangs from the front of the table and carries the initials of his new party name in capital letters.

Fenton Thank you. Any questions?

Reporter Can I ask you about the name of the party? United Kingdom One Country?

Fenton That's it, fella. Say it loud and clear.

Reporter So . . . UKOC?

Fenton Beg pardon?

Reporter UKOC. That's what it spells.

Fenton peers over the front of the table to check.

Fenton Aye, well, we're still working on the actual words and . . . letters and . . . that sort of . . . shit.

SCENE SEVENTEEN

The Prime Minister's office. Room is empty. His phone rings.

Soli (*from behind the bookcase*) Let it ring.

Anthea I can't. There's only me and the War Office have that number, and by a process of elimination . . .

Soli Business before pleasure, right?

Anthea (*answering the phone*) Yes?

Magnus (*on the other end*) Who's that?

Anthea Magnus? I won't ask how you got this number, but just for my peace of mind, you're not calling to say that Russia have invaded Finland?

Magnus Not as far as I'm aware. Is the, er, is your dad there?

Anthea No, he's off somewhere being all smug and self-congratulatory. Want to leave a message?

Magnus Just calling him to say thanks, for, you know, getting it all sorted. It's . . . appreciated.

Anthea Well, he put such a shift in, I mean absolutely pulled out all the stops, so he'll be happy to hear that all his hard work paid off.

Magnus OK. Anyway. Cheers. Oh by the way, I finished the book. Great ending.

Anthea Yes, that homecoming scene. Very sweet.

Magnus No I mean the bit with the shootings and the hangings. Loved it. Straight out of a top video game that stuff. You know, the revenge and the bloodletting. (*Pause.*) Imagine that.

Anthea Magnus, you do know it's just an old poem, don't you. Not meant to be taken . . . literally.

Magnus Metaphorical, right? I know all about that. Who doesn't love a good metaphor?

Anthea Magnus?

Magnus Be seeing you, then. Got a few ends to tie up.

Anthea Magnus? Magnus?

She redials.

Get me my father. (*Pause.*) Well, drag him out of the club and on to the fucking phone. I think we might have a little public relations problem about to unfold.

SCENE EIGHTEEN

The Smiths' family home.

Magnus puts down the phone, revealing that in his other hand he is carrying a serious-looking crossbow, loaded.

Magnus Right, gentlemen, if you could just shuffle your way over here for the final execution.

Prompted by the loaded crossbow, Kite and Reynolds shuffle across the hall. They are stripped to their underpants and have been bound at the hands and ankles with cable ties. The both have gaffer tape across their mouths.

That's it, gentlemen. That's very obliging.

Kite and Reynolds are both protesting as loudly as possible behind their gags. Magnus approaches Kite.

Any last requests?

He rips the tape from Kite's mouth, causing him to scream in agony.

Kite Ouch, bloody hell fire, that fucking hurt. You little wanker, I'll bloody well –

Magnus Oh, still not mended, let's pop the plaster back on till it's healed. What about you – any last words?

Seeing the pain that Kite went through, Reynolds shakes his head.

Very wise. (*To Kite.*) You see, I think your friend's learning his lesson. Now if you just want to relax there for a minute while I get the shot lined up.

Implying that he is going to shoot them with the crossbow, he walks to the far end of the hall, then reveals a video camera on a tripod.

That's nice. Really nice. Right in the crosshairs. OK, all set? Say cheese.

Magnus sets the camera going. He then produces a toy arrow with a sucker on the end, which he carries through the air in his hand, licks with his mouth, and

*sticks on Reynolds' forehead. From his pocket he then
produces a comedy arrow that appears to have gone
though someone's head, and puts it on Kite. He turns
to the camera.*

GOTCHA!

*He holds his position for a second for the purpose of
the film.*

Thanks so much, gentlemen. I'll get that loaded up
online and you'll be an internet sensation by breakfast.
All in the public interest, you understand.

And you'll be wanting all your equipment back. Really
grimy it was, clogged up with filth, so I've done a bit of
laundry for you.

*Magnus pulls up a washing line or creel, on which
hang several cameras, phones, microphones, etc., all
dripping with water.*

Gave them a really deep clean. Spotless now. Not a speck
of dirt anywhere. All part of the service.

SCENE NINETEEN

*Smith and Penelope's bedroom. Night. Smith and Penelope
are in bed. Penelope gets out of bed.*

Smith Stay with me.

Penelope I need a glass of water. Don't go anywhere.

*Smith notices a single flower in a vase on Penelope's
side of the bed. It is the moly flower.*

Smith Who got you the flower? One of your admirers?

Penelope It was in your pocket.

Smith Was it?

Penelope Thought you might have plucked it for me in some far-flung field.

Smith stares at the flower, as if it has broken a dream or triggered a vague memory. Penelope has gone into the bathroom. She is out of sight but can be heard, and the light from the bathroom door falls across the bed. She begins humming to herself. After a while, Smith recognises the tune as the song of the sirens.

Smith Penny? Penny?

We hear her turning the tap on. The sound of the water gets louder and louder until it is the sound of the sea. A window in the bedroom blows open and the wind howls through.

Penny. Penelope.

Smith reaches for a switch to turn the light on, but the light is the eyeball of the Cyclops, staring and blinking. Through the sound of wind and rain the squealing of pigs can be heard. The bed begins to pitch and roll like a boat in a storm.

PENELOPE. PENELOPE.

The End.